At Issue

I Vaccines

Other Books in the At Issue Series:

At Issue

| Vaccines

Noël Merino, Book Editor

GREENHAVEN PRESS
A part of Gale, Cengage Learning

GALE
CENGAGE Learning·

Farmington Hills, Mich • San Francisco • New York • Waterville, Maine
Meriden, Conn • Mason, Ohio • Chicago

Patricia Coryell, *Vice President & Publisher, New Products & GVRL*
Douglas Dentino, *Manager, New Products*
Judy Galens, *Acquisitions Editor*

For more information, contact:
Greenhaven Press
27500 Drake Rd.
Farmington Hills, MI 48331-3535
Or you can visit our Internet site at gale.cengage.com

Articles in Greenhaven Press anthologies are often edited for length to meet page requirements. In addition, original titles of these works are changed to clearly present the main thesis and to explicitly indicate the author's opinion. Every effort is made to ensure that Greenhaven Press accurately reflects the original intent of the authors. Every effort has been made to trace the owners of copyrighted material.

Cover photograph copyright © Images.com/Corbis.

LIBRARY OF CONGRESS CATALOGING-IN-PUBLICATION DATA

Vaccines / Noël Merino, book editor.
    pages cm. -- (At issue)
    Includes bibliographical references and index.
    ISBN 978-0-7377-7193-0 (hardcover) -- ISBN 978-0-7377-7194-7 (pbk.)
    1. Vaccines--Juvenile literature. 2. Vaccination--Juvenile literature. I. Merino, Noël, editor.
    RA638.V3313 2015
    614.4'7--dc23

                                                                    2014024408

Printed in the United States of America
1 2 3 4 5 6 7 18 17 16 15 14

Contents

Introduction

Vaccination is the process by which a weakened form of a particular disease is injected into a healthy person in order to get the body to develop antibodies to a particular virus or bacterium. For many diseases, exposure to the disease will cause the body to produce antibodies to resist infection a second time, thus making the person immune from getting the disease. The diseases for which vaccines are created have serious risks, so developing antibodies without getting the actual disease is the preferable route to immunity. Vaccines work by imitating an infection, causing the body to create antibodies to disease, thereby becoming immune to future infection. Today, dozens of vaccines are used worldwide in an attempt to create immunity to infectious diseases.

In the late eighteenth century, English scientist Edward Jenner created the first vaccine for smallpox by inoculating a boy with cowpox (the source of the word "vaccine," from its Latin root *vaccinia*). Over the next two centuries, with the implementation of mass smallpox vaccination, the disease was certified as eradicated in 1979 by the World Health Organization. It is one of only two diseases considered to have been eradicated by vaccination (the other being the cattle disease, rinderpest). However, vaccination over the last two centuries for dozens of diseases—including cholera, rabies, and tetanus—has corresponded with large reductions in incidence of these diseases.

The US Centers for Disease Control and Prevention (CDC) recommends vaccination for sixteen diseases: diphtheria, hepatitis A, hepatitis B, *Haemophilus influenzae* type b (Hib), human papillomavirus (HPV, for girls only), influenza, measles, meningococcal disease, mumps, pertussis (whooping cough), pneumococcal disease, polio, rotavirus, rubella, tetanus, and varicella (chickenpox). Because immunity for many of these diseases requires multiple injections, several dozen injections are recommended throughout childhood and into adulthood. Several of these recommended vaccines are relatively new: the hepatitis A and chickenpox vaccines first became available in 1995; the first rotavirus vaccine came out in 1998 (but was withdrawn in 1999 and replaced in 2006); and the HPV vaccine first became available in 2006.

The US government recommends certain vaccines for the general public, but it is the states that take charge of monitoring vaccination by requiring schoolchildren to have certain vaccines. In 1855, Massachusetts became the first state to mandate vaccination for schoolchildren, requiring that all children attending school be vaccinated against smallpox. Massachusetts later required that all citizens, including adults, be vaccinated against smallpox or face a fine. In 1905, after a Cambridge, Massachusetts, citizen challenged the law, the US Supreme Court in *Jacobson v. Massachusetts* upheld the mandate under the police power of the state. The Court reasoned, "Upon the principle of self-defense, of paramount necessity, a community has the right to protect itself against an epidemic of disease which threatens the safety of its members."

Schoolchildren are not the only group that is required by state law to be vaccinated against certain diseases. Employees of hospitals and nursing homes are frequently required to be vaccinated against diseases such as measles and mumps. In 2009, New York State implemented a temporary requirement that health-care workers get the influenza A (H1N1) vaccine because of the pandemic at that time.

No law requiring vaccination of schoolchildren or health-care workers constitutes a mandate without exception. All states allow exemptions to their school vaccination laws for medical reasons, all but two allow religious exemptions, and almost half permit philosophical opposition as grounds for exemption to vaccination requirements. Similar exemptions exist for the vaccination requirements of health-care workers.

Concern about the safety of vaccines has increased in recent years, correlating with an increase in the demand for religious and philosophical exemptions on the part of parents. Between 1991 and 2011, the average state-level nonmedical exemption rate doubled from about 1 percent of the population to approximately 2 percent. Including medical exemptions, the vaccination exemption rate has reached more than 10 percent in certain communities—although nationwide it is about 3 percent. Outbreaks of measles, polio, pertussis, and rubella have been documented in areas with high rates of unvaccinated children, causing concern that certain diseases once thought to be almost eliminated are now making a comeback.

The debate over vaccination continues. Disagreements about the safety and effectiveness of vaccines and disagreements about the rights of parents to exempt their children from vaccination requirements are a few of the current controversies explored in the viewpoints included in *At Issue: Vaccines*.

1

Vaccination Programs Have Reduced the Incidence of Many Diseases

Centers for Disease Control and Prevention

The US Centers for Disease Control and Prevention (CDC) serves as the federal government's national agency for developing and applying disease prevention and control, environmental health, and health promotion and health education activities designed to improve the health of the people of the United States.

Vaccination against a variety of diseases has been successful in reducing their incidence. The vaccines for diseases such as polio, measles, and pertussis have reduced the incidence of these diseases, preventing negative health effects and death. The vaccines for diseases such as rubella and hepatitis B have helped reduce long-term illnesses caused by these diseases. Even with diseases that have been mostly eliminated in the United States due to vaccination, such as diphtheria, continued vaccination remains important.

In the U.S., vaccines have reduced or eliminated many infectious diseases that once routinely killed or harmed many infants, children, and adults. However, the viruses and bacteria that cause vaccine-preventable disease and death still exist and can be passed on to people who are not protected by vaccines. Vaccine-preventable diseases have many social and economic

"What Would Happen If We Stopped Vaccinations?" Centers for Disease Control and Prevention (CDC), September 18, 2013.

costs: sick children miss school and can cause parents to lose time from work. These diseases also result in doctor's visits, hospitalizations, and even premature deaths.

The Impact of the Polio Vaccine

Stopping vaccination against polio will leave people susceptible to infection with poliovirus. Polio causes acute paralysis that can lead to permanent physical disability and even death. Before polio vaccine was available, 13,000 to 20,000 cases of paralytic polio were reported each year in the United States. Annual epidemics of polio often left victims—mostly children—in braces, crutches, wheelchairs, and, in serious cases, iron lungs. Many of the children that survived experienced life-long consequences from the disease.

In 1988, the World Health Assembly unanimously agreed to eradicate polio worldwide. As a result of global polio eradication efforts, the number of cases reported globally has decreased from more than 350,000 cases in 1988 to 187 cases in 2012 (as of November 14, 2012). Only three countries remain endemic for polio in 2012: Afghanistan, Nigeria, and Pakistan. Stopping vaccination before eradication is achieved would result in a resurgence of this preventable disease and threaten future generations of children.

More than 90 percent of people who are not immune will get measles if they are exposed to the virus.

The Importance of Measles Vaccination

Before measles immunization was available, nearly everyone in the U.S. got measles. An average of 450 measles-associated deaths were reported each year between 1953 and 1963.

In the U.S., *up to 20 percent of persons with measles are hospitalized.* Seventeen percent of measles cases have had one or more complications, such as ear infections, pneumonia, or diarrhea. Pneumonia is present in about six percent of cases and accounts for most of the measles deaths. Although less common, some persons with measles develop encephalitis (swelling of the lining of the brain), resulting in brain damage.

As many as three of every 1,000 persons with measles will die in the U.S. In the developing world, the rate is much higher, with death occurring in about one of every 100 persons with measles.

Measles is one of the most infectious diseases in the world and is frequently imported into the U.S. In the period 1997–2000, most cases were associated with international visitors or U.S. residents who were exposed to the measles virus while traveling abroad. More than 90 percent of people who are not immune will get measles if they are exposed to the virus.

According to the World Health Organization (WHO), nearly 900,000 measles-related deaths occurred among persons in developing countries in 1999. In populations that are not immune to measles, measles spreads rapidly. *If vaccinations were stopped, each year about 2.7 million measles deaths worldwide could be expected.*

In the U.S., widespread use of measles vaccine has led to a greater than 99 percent reduction in measles compared with the pre-vaccine era. If we stopped immunization, measles would increase to pre-vaccine levels.

The Impact of the *Haemophilus Influenzae* Type b (Hib) Vaccine

Before Hib vaccine became available, Hib was the most common cause of bacterial meningitis in U.S. infants and children. Before the vaccine was developed, there were approximately 20,000 invasive Hib cases annually. Approximately two-thirds of the 20,000 cases were meningitis, and one-third were other life-threatening invasive Hib diseases such as bacteria in the blood, pneumonia, or inflammation of the epiglottis.

About one of every 200 U.S. children under 5 years of age got an invasive Hib disease. *Hib meningitis once killed 600 children each year and left many survivors with deafness, seizures, or mental retardation.*

Since introduction of conjugate Hib vaccine in December 1987, the incidence of Hib has declined by 98 percent. From 1994–1998, fewer than 10 fatal cases of invasive Hib disease were reported each year.

This preventable disease was a common, devastating illness as recently as 1990; now, most pediatricians just finishing training have never seen a case. If we were to stop immunization, we would likely soon return to the pre-vaccine numbers of invasive Hib disease cases and deaths.

The Danger of Stopping Pertussis Vaccination

Since the early 1980s, reported pertussis cases have been increasing, with peaks every 3–5 years; however, the number of reported cases remains much lower than levels seen in the pre-vaccine era. Compared with pertussis cases in other age groups, infants who are 6 months old or younger with pertussis experience the highest rate of hospitalization, pneumonia, seizures, encephalopathy (a degenerative disease of the brain) and death. From 2000 through 2012, 255 persons died from pertussis; 228 of these were less than six months old.

Before pertussis immunizations were available, nearly all children developed whooping cough. In the U.S., prior to pertussis immunization, between 150,000 and 260,000 cases of pertussis were reported each year, with up to 9,000 pertussis-related deaths.

Pertussis can be a severe illness, resulting in prolonged coughing spells that can last for many weeks. These spells can make it difficult for a person to eat, drink, and breathe. Because vomiting often occurs after a coughing spell, persons may lose weight and become dehydrated. In infants, *it can also cause pneumonia and lead to brain damage, seizures, and mental retardation.*

If we stopped pertussis immunizations in the U.S., we would experience a massive resurgence of pertussis disease.

The newer pertussis vaccine (acellular or DTaP) has been available for use in the United States since 1991 and has been recommended for exclusive use since 1998. These vaccines are effective and associated with fewer mild and moderate adverse reactions when compared with the older (whole-cell DTP) vaccines.

During the 1970s, widespread concerns about the safety of the older pertussis vaccine led to a rapid fall in immunization levels in the United Kingdom. More than 100,000 cases and 36 deaths due to pertussis were reported during an epidemic in the mid 1970s. In Japan, pertussis vaccination coverage fell from 80 percent in 1974 to 20 percent in 1979. An epidemic occurred in 1979, resulting in more than 13,000 cases and 41 deaths.

Pertussis cases occur throughout the world. If we stopped pertussis immunizations in the U.S., we would experience a massive resurgence of pertussis disease. *A study found that, in eight countries where immunization coverage was reduced, incidence rates of pertussis surged to 10 to 100 times the rates in countries where vaccination rates were sustained.*

The Long-Term Risks of Pneumococcus and Rubella

Before pneumococcal conjugate vaccine became available for children, pneumococcus caused 63,000 cases of invasive pneumococcal disease and 6,100 deaths in the U.S. each year. Many children who developed pneumococcal meningitis also developed long-term complications such as deafness or seizures. Since the vaccine was introduced, the incidence rate of invasive pneumococcal disease in children has been reduced by about 85%. Pneumococcal conjugate vaccine also reduces spread of pneumococcus from children to adults. In 2011 alone, there were 35,000 fewer cases of invasive pneumococcal disease caused by strains included in the vaccine, including 21,000 fewer cases in children and adults too old to receive the vaccine. If we were to stop immunization, we would likely soon return to the pre-vaccine numbers of invasive pneumococcal disease cases and deaths.

While rubella is usually mild in children and adults, up to 90 percent of infants born to mothers infected with rubella during the first trimester of pregnancy will develop *congenital rubella syndrome (CRS), resulting in heart defects, cataracts, mental retardation, and deafness.*

In 1964–1965, before rubella immunization was used routinely in the U.S., there was an epidemic of rubella that resulted in an estimated 20,000 infants born with CRS, with 2,100 neonatal deaths and 11,250 miscarriages. Of the 20,000 infants born with CRS, 11,600 were deaf, 3,580 were blind, and 1,800 were mentally retarded.

Due to the widespread use of rubella vaccine, only six CRS cases were provisionally reported in the U.S. in 2000. Because many developing countries do not include rubella in the childhood immunization schedule, many of these cases occurred in foreign-born adults. Since 1996, greater than 50 percent of the reported rubella cases have been among adults. Since 1999, there have been 40 pregnant women infected with rubella.

If we stopped rubella immunization, immunity to rubella would decline and rubella would once again return, resulting in pregnant women becoming infected with rubella and then giving birth to infants with CRS.

The Impact of the Chickenpox Vaccine

Prior to the licensing of the chickenpox vaccine in 1995, almost all persons in the United States had suffered from chickenpox by adulthood. Each year, the virus caused an estimated 4 million cases of chickenpox, 11,000 hospitalizations, and 100–150 deaths.

A highly contagious disease, chickenpox is usually mild but can be severe in some persons. Infants, adolescents and adults, pregnant women, and immunocompromised persons are at particular risk for serious complications including secondary bacterial infections, loss of fluids (dehydration), pneumonia, and central nervous system involvement. The availability of the chickenpox vaccine and its subsequent widespread use has had a major impact on reducing cases of chickenpox and related morbidity, hospitalizations, and deaths. In some areas, cases have decreased as much as 90% over prevaccination numbers.

About 5,000 persons will die each year from hepatitis B-related liver disease resulting in over $700 million in medical and work loss costs.

If vaccination against chickenpox were to stop, the disease would eventually return to prevaccination rates, with virtually all susceptible persons becoming infected with the virus at some point in their lives.

The Danger of Hepatitis B Infection

More than 2 billion persons worldwide have been infected with the hepatitis B virus at some time in their lives. Of these, 350 million are life-long carriers of the disease and can transmit the virus to others. *One million of these people die each year from liver disease and liver cancer.*

National studies have shown that about 12.5 million Americans have been infected with hepatitis B virus at some point in their lifetime. One and one quarter million Americans are estimated to have chronic (long-lasting) infection, of whom 20 percent to 30 percent acquired their infection in childhood. Chronic hepatitis B virus infection increases a person's risk for chronic liver disease, cirrhosis, and liver cancer. About 5,000 persons will die each year from hepatitis B-related liver disease resulting in over $700 million in medical and work loss costs.

The number of new infections per year has declined from an average of 450,000 in the 1980s to about 80,000 in 1999. The greatest decline has occurred among children and adolescents due to routine hepatitis B vaccination.

Infants and children who become infected with hepatitis B virus are at highest risk of developing lifelong infection, which often leads to death from liver disease (cirrhosis) and liver cancer.

Approximately 25 percent of children who become infected with life-long hepatitis B virus would be expected to die of related liver disease as adults.

CDC [Centers for Disease Control and Prevention] estimates that one-third of the life-long hepatitis B virus infections in the United States resulted from infections occurring in infants and young children. About 16,000–20,000 hepatitis B antigen infected women give birth each year in the United States. It is estimated that 12,000 children born to hepatitis B virus infected mothers were infected each year before implementation of infant immunization programs. In addition, approximately 33,000 children (10 years of age and younger) of mothers who are not infected with hepatitis B virus were infected each year before routine recommendation of childhood hepatitis B vaccination.

The Importance of Diphtheria Vaccination

Diphtheria is a serious disease caused by a bacterium. This germ produces a poisonous substance or toxin which frequently causes heart and nerve problems. The case fatality rate is 5 percent to 10 percent, with higher case-fatality rates (up to 20 percent) in children younger than 5 and adults older than 40 years of age.

In the 1920s, diphtheria was a major cause of illness and death for children in the U.S. In 1921, a total of 206,000 cases and 15,520 deaths were reported. With vaccine development in 1923, new cases of diphtheria began to fall in the U.S. In the past decade, there were less than five cases of diphtheria in the U.S. reported to CDC.

Although diphtheria is rare in the U.S., it appears that the bacteria continue to get passed among people. In 1996, 10 isolates (samples) of the bacteria were obtained from people in an American Indian community in South Dakota, none of whom had classic diphtheria disease. There was one death reported in 2003 from clinical diphtheria in a 63-year-old male who had never been vaccinated.

There are high rates of susceptibility among adults. Screening tests conducted since 1977 show that somewhere between 4 to 8 out of every 10 adults over the age of 60 are no longer protected against diphtheria.

Diphtheria is common in other parts of the world and with the increase in international travel, *diphtheria and other infectious diseases are only a plane ride away.* If we stopped immunization, the U.S. might experience a situation similar to the Newly Independent States of the former Soviet Union. With the breakdown of the public health services in this area, diphtheria epidemics began in 1990, fueled primarily by people who were not properly vaccinated. From 1990–1999, more than 150,000 cases and 5,000 deaths were reported.

The Danger of Tetanus (Lockjaw)

Tetanus is a severe, often fatal disease. The bacteria that cause tetanus are widely distributed in soil and street dust, are found in the waste of many animals, and are very resistant to heat

and germ-killing cleaners. From 1922–1926, there were an estimated 1,314 cases of tetanus per year in the U.S. In the late
1940's, the tetanus vaccine was introduced, and tetanus became a disease that was officially counted and tracked by public health officials. In 2000, only 41 cases of tetanus were reported in the U.S.

Every year tetanus kills 300,000 newborns and 30,000
birth mothers who were not properly vaccinated.

People who get tetanus suffer from stiffness and spasms of
the muscles. The larynx (throat) can close causing breathing
and eating difficulties, muscles spasms can cause fractures
(breaks) of the spine and long bones, and some people go
into a coma, and die. *Approximately 20 percent of reported
cases end in death.*

Tetanus in the U.S. is primarily a disease of adults, but unvaccinated children and infants of unvaccinated mothers are
also at risk for tetanus and neonatal tetanus, respectively.
From 1995–1997, 33 percent of reported cases of tetanus occurred among persons 60 years of age or older and 60 percent
occurred in patients greater than 40 years of age. The National
Health Interview Survey found that in 1995, only 36 percent
of adults 65 or older had received a tetanus vaccination during the preceding 10 years.

Worldwide, tetanus in newborn infants continues to be a
huge problem. Every year *tetanus kills 300,000 newborns and
30,000 birth mothers who were not properly vaccinated.* Even
though the number of reported cases is low, an increased
number of tetanus cases in younger persons has been observed recently in the U.S. among intravenous drug users, particularly heroin users.

Tetanus is infectious, but not contagious, so unlike other
vaccine-preventable diseases, immunization by members of
the community will not protect others from the disease. Be-

cause tetanus bacteria are widespread in the environment, tetanus can only be prevented by immunization. If vaccination against tetanus were stopped, persons of all ages in the U.S. would be susceptible to this serious disease.

The Impact of the Mumps Vaccine

Before the mumps vaccine was introduced, mumps was a major cause of deafness in children, occurring in approximately 1 in 20,000 reported cases. Mumps is usually a mild viral disease. However, serious complications, such as inflammation of the brain (encephalitis) can occur rarely. Prior to mumps vaccine, mumps encephalitis was the leading cause of viral encephalitis in the United States, but is now rarely seen.

Serious side effects of mumps are more common among adults than children. Swelling of the testes is the most common side effect in males past the age of puberty, occurring in up to 37 percent of post-pubertal males who contract mumps. *An increase in miscarriages has been found among women who develop mumps during the first trimester of pregnancy.*

Before there was a vaccine against mumps, mumps was a very common disease in U.S. children, with as many as 300,000 cases reported every year. After vaccine licensure in 1967, reports of mumps decreased rapidly. In 1986 and 1987, there was a resurgence of mumps with 12,848 cases reported in 1987. Since 1989, the incidence of mumps has declined, with 266 reported cases in 2001. This recent decrease is probably due to the fact that children have received a second dose of mumps vaccine (part of the two-dose schedule for measles, mumps, rubella or MMR). Studies have shown that the effectiveness of mumps vaccine ranges from 73% to 91% after 1 dose and from 79% to 95% after 2 doses and that 2 doses are more effective than 1 dose.

We can not let our guard down against mumps. A 2006 outbreak among college students led to over 6,500 cases and a 2009–10 outbreak in the tradition-observant Jewish community in 2 states led to over 3,400 cases. Mumps is a communicable disease and while prolonged close contact among persons may facilitate transmission, maintenance of high 2-dose MMR vaccine coverage remains the most effective way to prevent and limit the size of mumps outbreaks.

2

Opposition to Vaccines Has Existed as Long as Vaccination Itself

The History of Vaccines, The College of Physicians of Philadelphia

The History of Vaccines is an award-winning informational, educational website created by the College of Physicians of Philadelphia, one of the oldest medical societies in the United States.

Shortly after the first widespread vaccination began, there have existed opposition movements to the use of vaccines. In the 1800s, smallpox vaccination was opposed in the United Kingdom. When vaccination became widespread in the United States, similar antivaccination leagues were formed. Recent antivaccination movements include opposition to the diphtheria, tetanus, and pertussis vaccine in the 1970s and 1980s, and opposition to the measles, mumps, and rubella vaccine starting in the 1990s.

Health and medicine scholars have described vaccination as one of the top ten achievements of public health in the 20th century. Yet, opposition to vaccination has existed as long as vaccination itself. Critics of vaccination have taken a variety of positions, including opposition to the smallpox vaccine in England and the United States in the mid to late 1800s, and the resulting anti-vaccination leagues; as well as more recent vaccination controversies such as those surrounding the safety and efficacy of the diphtheria, tetanus, and pertussis (DTP) immunization, the measles, mumps, and rubella (MMR) vaccine, and the use of a mercury-containing preservative called thimerosal.

Smallpox and the Anti-Vaccination Leagues in England

Widespread smallpox vaccination began in the early 1800s, following Edward Jenner's cowpox experiments, in which he showed that he could protect a child from smallpox if he infected him or her with lymph from a cowpox blister. Jenner's ideas were novel for his time, however, and they were met with immediate public criticism. The rationale for this criticism varied, and included sanitary, religious, scientific, and political objections.

The Vaccination Act of 1898 removed penalties and included a "conscientious objector" clause, so that parents who did not believe in vaccination's safety or efficacy could obtain an exemption certificate.

For some parents, the smallpox vaccination itself induced fear and protest. It included scoring the flesh on a child's arm, and inserting lymph from the blister of a person who had been vaccinated about a week earlier. Some objectors, including the local clergy, believed that the vaccine was "unchristian" because it came from an animal. For other anti-vaccinators, their discontent with the smallpox vaccine reflected their general distrust in medicine and in Jenner's ideas about disease spread. Suspicious of the vaccine's efficacy, some skeptics alleged that smallpox resulted from decaying matter in the atmosphere. Lastly, many people objected to vaccination because they believed it violated their personal liberty, a tension that worsened as the government developed mandatory vaccine policies.

The Vaccination Act of 1853 ordered mandatory vaccination for infants up to 3 months old, and the Act of 1867 extended this age requirement to 14 years, adding penalties for vaccine refusal. The laws were met with immediate resistance from citizens who demanded the right to control their bodies and those of their children. The Anti Vaccination League and the Anti-Compulsory Vaccination League formed in response to the mandatory laws, and numerous anti-vaccination journals sprang up.

The town of Leicester [England, United Kingdom] was a particular hotbed of anti vaccine activity and the site of many anti-vaccine rallies. The local paper [according to S. Williamson] described the details of a rally: "An escort was formed, preceded by a banner, to escort a young mother and two men, all of whom had resolved to give themselves up to the police and undergo imprisonment in preference to having their children vaccinated. . . . The three were attended by a numerous crowd . . . three hearty cheers were given for them, which were renewed with increased vigor as they entered the doors of the police cells." The Leicester Demonstration March of 1885 was one of the most notorious anti-vaccination demonstrations. There, 80,000–100,000 anti-vaccinators led an elaborate march, complete with banners, a child's coffin, and an effigy of Jenner.

Such demonstrations and general vaccine opposition lead to the development of a commission designed to study vaccination. In 1896 the commission ruled that vaccination protected against smallpox, but suggested removing penalties for failure to vaccinate. The Vaccination Act of 1898 removed penalties and included a "conscientious objector" clause, so that parents who did not believe in vaccination's safety or efficacy could obtain an exemption certificate.

Smallpox and the Anti-vaccination Leagues in the United States

Toward the end of the 19th century, smallpox outbreaks in the United States led to vaccine campaigns and related anti-vaccine activity. The Anti Vaccination Society of America was founded in 1879, following a visit to America by leading British anti-vaccinationist William Tebb. Two other leagues, the New England Anti Compulsory Vaccination League (1882) and the Anti-vaccination League of New York City (1885) followed. The American anti-vaccinationists waged court battles to repeal vaccination laws in several states including California, Illinois, and Wisconsin.

In 1902, following a smallpox outbreak, the board of health of the city of Cambridge, Massachusetts, mandated all city residents to be vaccinated against smallpox. City resident Henning Jacobson refused vaccination on the grounds that the law violated his right to care for his own body how he knew best. In turn, the city filed criminal charges against him. After losing his court battle locally, Jacobson appealed to the U.S. Supreme Court. In 1905 the Court found in the state's favor, ruling that the state could enact compulsory laws to protect the public in the event of a communicable disease. This was the first U.S. Supreme Court case concerning the power of states in public health law.

The Diphtheria, Tetanus, and Pertussis (DTP) Vaccine Controversy

Anti-vaccination positions and vaccination controversies are not limited to the past. In the mid 1970s, an international controversy over the safety of the DTP immunization erupted in Europe, Asia, Australia, and North America. In the United Kingdom (UK), opposition resulted in response to a report from the Great Ormond Street Hospital for Sick Children in London, alleging that 36 children suffered neurological conditions following DTP immunization. Television documentaries and newspaper reports drew public attention to the controversy. An advocacy group, The Association of Parents of Vaccine Damaged Children (APVDC), also piqued public interest in the potential risks and consequences of DTP.

In response to decreased vaccination rates and three major epidemics of whooping cough (pertussis), the Joint Commission on Vaccination and Immunization (JCVI), an independent expert advisory committee in the UK, confirmed the safety of the immunization. Nonetheless, public confusion continued, in part because of diverse opinions within the medical profession. For example, surveys of medical providers in the UK in the late 1970s found that they were reluctant to recommend the immunization to all patients. Additionally, an outspoken physician and vaccine opponent, Gordon Stewart, published a series of case reports linking neurological disorders to DTP, sparking additional debate. In response, the JCVI launched the National Childhood Encephalopathy Study (NCES). The study identified every child between 2 and 36 months hospitalized in the UK for neurological illness, and assessed whether or not the immunization was associated with increased risk. NCES results indicated that the risk was very low, and this data lent support to a national pro-immunization campaign. Members of the APVDC continued to argue in court for recognition and compensation, but were denied both due to the lack of evidence linking the DTP immunization with harm.

The U.S. controversy began with media attention on the alleged risks of DTP. A 1982 documentary, *DPT: Vaccination Roulette*, described alleged adverse reactions to the immunization and minimized the benefits. Similarly, a 1991 book titled *A Shot in the Dark* outlined potential risks. As in the UK, concerned and angry parents formed victim advocacy groups, but the counter response from medical organizations, like the Academy of Pediatrics and the Centers for Disease Control and Prevention, was stronger in the United States. Although the media storm instigated several lawsuits against vaccine manufacturers, increased vaccine prices, and caused some companies to stop making DTP, the overall controversy affected immunization rates less than in the UK.

A large number of research studies have been conducted to assess the safety of the MMR vaccine, and none of them has found a link between the vaccine and autism.

The Measles, Mumps, and Rubella (MMR) Vaccine Controversy

Nearly 25 years after the DTP controversy, England was again the site of anti-vaccination activity, this time regarding the MMR vaccine.

In 1998, British doctor Andrew Wakefield recommended further investigation of a possible relationship between bowel disease, autism, and the MMR vaccine. A few years later, Wakefield alleged the vaccine was not properly tested before being put into use. The media seized these stories, igniting public fear and confusion over the safety of the vaccine. The *Lancet*, the journal that originally published Wakefield's work, stated in 2004 that it should not have published the paper. The General Medical Council, an independent regulator for doctors in the UK, found that Wakefield had a "fatal conflict of interest." He had been paid by a law board to find out if there was evidence to support a litigation case by parents who believed that the vaccine had harmed their children. In 2010, the *Lancet* formally retracted the paper after the British General Medical Council ruled against Wakefield in several areas. Wakefield was struck from the medical register in Great Britain and may no longer practice medicine there. In January 2011, *The BMJ* published a series of reports by journalist Brian Deer outlining evidence that Wakefield had committed scientific fraud by falsifying data and also that Wakefield hoped to financially profit from his investigations in several ways.

A large number of research studies have been conducted to assess the safety of the MMR vaccine, and none of them has found a link between the vaccine and autism.

The Thimerosal Controversy

Thimerosal, a mercury containing compound used as a preservative in vaccines, has also been the center of a vaccination and autism controversy. Although there is no clear scientific evidence that small amounts of thimerosal in vaccines cause harm, in July 1999, leading U.S. public health and medical organizations and vaccine manufacturers agreed that thimerosal should be reduced or eliminated from vaccines as a precautionary measure. In 2001, The Institute of Medicine's Immunization Safety Review Committee issued a report concluding that there was not enough evidence to *prove* or *disprove* claims that thimerosal in childhood vaccines causes autism, attention deficit hypersensitivity disorder, or speech or language delay. A more recent report by the committee "favors rejection of a causal relationship between thimerosal-containing vaccines and autism." Even with this finding, some researchers continue to study the possible links between thimerosal and autism.

Despite scientific evidence, concerns over thimerosal have led to a public "Green Our Vaccines" campaign, a movement to remove "toxins" from vaccines, for fear that these substances lead to autism. Celebrity Jenny McCarthy, her advocacy group Generation Rescue, and the organization Talk about Curing Autism (TACA) have spearheaded these efforts.

Although the time periods have changed, the emotions and deep-rooted beliefs—whether philosophical, political, or spiritual—that underlie vaccine opposition have remained relatively consistent since Edward Jenner introduced vaccination.

3

The Benefits of Vaccination Outweigh the Risks

The Children's Hospital of Philadelphia Vaccine Education Center

The Children's Hospital of Philadelphia Vaccine Education Center seeks to provide information about vaccines and the diseases they prevent to parents and healthcare professionals.

Although no vaccine is completely harmless, vaccines do protect people from the real danger of disease. The vaccines against hepatitis B, pertussis, pneumococcal disease, and rotavirus all have the possibility of certain side effects, but the harms of disease prevented by the vaccines outweigh the risk of any adverse effects. There are systems in place to protect against side effects and vaccines are only given to children after a long approval process.

The first definition of the word safe is "harmless." This definition would imply that any negative consequence of a vaccine would make the vaccine unsafe. Using this definition, no vaccine is 100 percent safe. Almost all vaccines can cause pain, redness or tenderness at the site of injection. And some vaccines cause more severe side effects. For example, the pertussis (or whooping cough) vaccine can cause persistent, inconsolable crying, high fever or seizures associated with fever. Although none of these severe symptoms result in permanent damage, they can be quite frightening to parents.

But, in truth, few things meet the definition of "harmless." Even everyday activities contain hidden dangers. For example, every year in the United States, 350 people are killed in bath- or shower-related accidents, 200 people are killed when food lodges in their windpipe, and 100 people are struck and killed by lightning. However, few of us consider eating solid food, taking a bath, or walking outside on a rainy day as unsafe activities. We just figure that the benefits of the activity clearly outweigh the risks.

Because the benefits of the hepatitis B vaccine clearly and definitively outweigh its risks, the hepatitis B vaccine is safe.

The second definition of the word safe is "having been preserved from a real danger." Using this definition, the danger (the disease) must be significantly greater than the means of protecting against the danger (the vaccine). Or, said another way, a vaccine's benefits must clearly and definitively outweigh its risks.

To better understand the definition of the word *safe* when applied to vaccines, let's examine four different vaccines and the diseases they prevent:

The Safety of the Hepatitis B Vaccine

The hepatitis B vaccine has few side effects. However, one side effect is serious. About one of every 600,000 doses of hepatitis B vaccine is complicated by a severe allergic reaction called anaphylaxis. The symptoms of anaphylaxis are hives, difficulty breathing and a drop in blood pressure. Although no one has ever died because of the hepatitis B vaccine, the symptoms of anaphylaxis caused by the vaccine can be quite frightening.

On the other hand, every year about 5,000 people die soon after being infected with hepatitis B virus. In addition, about 10,000 people every year suffer severe liver damage (called cirrhosis) or liver cancer caused by hepatitis B virus. People are much more likely to develop these severe and often fatal consequences of hepatitis B virus infection if they get infected when they are very young children. For this reason, the hepatitis B vaccine is recommended for newborns.

Some parents wonder whether it is necessary to give the hepatitis B virus vaccine to newborns. They ask: "How is a baby going to catch hepatitis B?" But, before the hepatitis B virus vaccine, every year in the United States about 18,000 children less than 10 years of age caught hepatitis B virus from someone other than their mother. Some children catch it from another family member, and some children catch it from someone outside the home who comes in contact with the baby. About 1 million people in the United States are infected with hepatitis B virus. However, because hepatitis B virus can cause a silent infection (meaning without obvious symptoms), many people who are infected with hepatitis B virus don't know that they have it! So it can be hard to tell from whom you could catch hepatitis B virus. Worse yet, many people don't realize that you can catch hepatitis B virus after coming into contact with minute quantities of blood through casual contact with someone who is infected (for example, sharing washcloths or toothbrushes). In fact, a milliliter of blood (about one-fifth of a teaspoon) from someone who is infected can contain as many as one billion infectious viruses, so people can be infected with quantities of infected blood small enough that they are not visible to the naked eye.

Because the benefits of the hepatitis B vaccine clearly and definitively outweigh its risks, the hepatitis B vaccine is safe.

The Safety of the Pertussis Vaccine

The old pertussis vaccine had far more risks than the hepatitis B vaccine. The old pertussis vaccine was called the "whole-cell" vaccine and had a high rate of severe side effects. Persistent, inconsolable crying occurred in one of every 100 doses, fever greater than 105 degrees occurred in one of every 330 doses, and seizures with fever occurred in one of every 1,750 doses. Due to negative publicity related to this vaccine, its use decreased in many areas of the world.

For example, the Japanese Ministry of Health decided to stop using the pertussis vaccine in 1975. In the three years before the vaccine was discontinued, there were 400 cases of pertussis and 10 deaths from pertussis in Japan. In the three years after the pertussis vaccine was discontinued, there were 13,000 cases of pertussis and 113 deaths! It should be noted that although the side effects of the pertussis vaccine were high, children didn't die from pertussis vaccine; however, they did die from pertussis infection. The Japanese Ministry of Health, realizing how costly their error had been, soon reinstituted the use of pertussis vaccine.

The children of Japan proved that, despite the side effects, the benefits of the old pertussis vaccine clearly outweighed the risks.

Scientific progress eventually led to the creation of another version of the pertussis vaccine. Known as the "acellular" pertussis vaccine, it was more purified, so instead of containing about 3,000 immunogenic proteins, it only contained two to five proteins. The ("acellular") pertussis vaccine became available in the United States in 1996. Children who received this vaccine had a much lower risk of severe side effects than those who received the old "whole-cell" vaccine. Therefore, the new pertussis vaccine is safer than the old pertussis vaccine. But because the benefits of the old pertussis vaccine outweighed its risks, it too was safe.

The Safety of the Pneumococcal Vaccine

Let's take a look at the pneumococcal vaccine. The pneumococcal vaccine was licensed in the United States in the year 2000 and was recommended for use in all children less than 5 years of age. Some parents chose to take a "wait-and-see" attitude. They reasoned that because the problems with the rotavirus vaccine were not revealed until the vaccine was given to 1 million children, why not wait and see what happened after the pneumococcal vaccine was given to several million or more children.

The first rotavirus vaccine was withdrawn from use because of a problem with safety.

However, the choice not to give the pneumococcal vaccine was not a risk-free choice. Before pneumococcal vaccine was first given to infants in 2000, every year in the United States about 700 children (less than 5 years old) got meningitis, 17,000 got bloodstream infections, and 71,000 got pneumonia from pneumococcus. So the choice not to give a pneumococcal vaccine was a choice to risk the severe, often permanent, and occasionally fatal consequences of pneumococcal infection. Parents should be reassured by two facts. First, the pneumococcal vaccine was tested in about 20,000 children before it was licensed for use. Second, the *Haemophilus influenzae* type b (Hib) vaccine is made in a manner almost identical to the pneumococcal vaccine and has been given safely to millions of children since 1990.

The Safety of the Rotavirus Vaccine

A new rotavirus vaccine was recommended for use in February 2006. This vaccine was tested in more than 70,000 infants. About half of the children received vaccine and the other half received a salt water solution. This large study showed the vaccine to be safe. Children who received the vaccine were not more likely to experience vomiting, diarrhea, fever, irritability or poor feeding than children who did not receive the vaccine.

The first rotavirus vaccine was withdrawn from use because of a problem with safety. The vaccine was found to cause a rare, but potentially very serious, side effect called intussusception. Intussusception occurs when one section of the small intestine folds into another section of the intestine. When this happens, the intestine can become blocked. Intussusception is a medical emergency, and children can die from the disease. The rotavirus vaccine was given to about 1 million children in the United States between 1998 and 1999. About one of every 10,000 children who were given the vaccine got intussusception (a total of about 100 children), and one child died because of the vaccine.

Because of the problem with intussusception in the previous vaccine, any new rotavirus vaccine had to be evaluated for this potential side effect as well. There are currently two rotavirus vaccines available in the U.S. Studies have shown that children who receive either of the rotavirus vaccines are no more likely to experience intussusception than those who did not receive the vaccine. Intussusception occurs naturally in about 1 of every 100,000 infants.

Systems in Place to Protect Against Side Effects

The previous rotavirus vaccine is an example of how rare side effects can be detected quickly. The rotavirus vaccine was tested in about 11,000 children before it was submitted to the FDA [US Food and Drug Administration] for licensure. After the vaccine was licensed and recommended for use, the vaccine was given to about 1 million children.

A system called the Vaccines Adverse Event Reporting System (VAERS) initially found about 15 cases of an intestinal blockage called intussusception soon after administration of the vaccine. This was worrisome enough to the Centers for Disease Control and Prevention (CDC) to cause them to temporarily suspend use of the rotavirus vaccine until it could be determined whether the vaccine did, in fact, cause intussusception. Their analysis showed that intussusception occurred in about one of every 10,000 children who received the vaccine. Because only 11,000 children were tested before the vaccine was licensed, it was really not possible to pick up such a rare side effect. The result of the rotavirus vaccine experience is that at least 60,000 children had to be tested before the next vaccine was licensed.

Several other systems of study to understand the rate of vaccine side effects, such as the Vaccine Safety Data Link (VSD), are also available. The VSD also allows one to determine the background rate of side effects, meaning the rate of adverse events in children who don't receive a vaccine. So, in many ways, systems like the Vaccine Safety Data Link are better than VAERS because they allow one to determine whether a particular vaccine is the cause of a rare side effect.

Trials can take years, giving companies ample time to provide the FDA with proof of long-term safety and effectiveness.

The Licensure of New Vaccines

Vaccines are only given to children after a long and careful review by a number of different groups. These different groups either: license, recommend or require vaccines.

The first of three processes, licensure, involves gaining approval from the Food and Drug Administration (FDA). As a result, it is the longest of these processes. It can take years, even decades, before pharmaceutical companies can actually start providing the vaccine. For example, the varicella [chicken pox] vaccine took about 11 years to be licensed by the FDA.

Vaccines are usually made by first showing that they are safe and effective in experimental animals. Once this is established, the vaccine becomes an Investigational New Drug (IND) and the company is given an IND license to further study the safety and effectiveness of the vaccine in adults, and eventually, children. Again, these trials can take years, giving companies ample time to provide the FDA with proof of long-term safety and effectiveness.

The Recommendation Process

The "recommendation" process begins only after a vaccine is licensed by the FDA. Doctors don't just decide to start giving the vaccine on their own. They seek the recommendations of the Advisory Committee on Immunization Practices (ACIP), which is part of the Centers for Disease Control and Prevention (CDC), the Committee on Infectious Diseases of the American Academy of Pediatrics (AAP), and the American Academy of Family Physicians (AAFP).

While the FDA licensure process involves determining the risks versus the benefits of a particular vaccine, the recommendation process considers the costs versus the benefits. Here's the distinction:

- The FDA examines vaccine safety by considering whether there are any risks (negative effects) associated with the vaccine. They ask: "Do these risks outweigh the benefits of the vaccine or vice versa?"

- In addition to considering the risks and benefits of a vaccine, the ACIP, AAP and AAFP also examine the costs associated with immunizing all or just a segment of the population. For instance, with the chickenpox (varicella) vaccine: What is the cost of immunizing children compared with the potential savings in medical and non-medical costs from immunizing them? (An example of non-medical costs would be money lost by parents who miss work taking care of their unvaccinated child.)

- Another part of the recommendation process is determining which groups of people within the population would benefit from the vaccine, and on what schedule the vaccine should be given based on data previously presented to the FDA.

Just because a vaccine is recommended for use doesn't mean that it is required for use. State legislatures and health departments determine whether a vaccine is required. They examine the practicality of requiring it for every child within the state. Factored into this equation is whether a local or state government can afford to pay for the vaccines of children whose parents can't afford it.

Whereas immunity from disease often follows a single natural infection, immunity from vaccines usually occurs only after several doses.

The Need for Vaccines

We still need vaccines for the following reasons:

- Some diseases are still so common that a choice not to get a vaccine is a choice to risk natural infection. Examples of these diseases include chickenpox, pertussis, hepatitis B, influenza and pneumococcus.

- Some diseases still occur in the United States at very low levels, so if immunization rates dropped even a little bit, outbreaks of disease would sweep across the country rapidly. Examples of these diseases include measles, mumps and Hib.

- Some diseases have been virtually eliminated from the United States, but still occur frequently in other parts of the world. Because international travel is common, it is quite possible for the disease to come to the US or for us to go to a place where the disease exists. Examples of these diseases include polio, rubella and diphtheria.

- Tetanus is the only vaccine against a disease that is not passed from one person to another. We can never eliminate tetanus from the environment, so this vaccine will always be required. . . .

It is true that natural infection almost always causes better immunity than vaccines. Whereas immunity from disease often follows a single natural infection, immunity from vaccines usually occurs only after several doses. However, the difference between vaccination and natural infection is the price paid for immunity.

The price paid for immunity after natural infection might be pneumonia from chickenpox, mental retardation from *Haemophilus influenzae* type b (Hib), pneumonia from pneumococcus, birth defects from rubella, liver cancer from hepatitis B virus, or death from measles.

Immunization with vaccines, like natural infections, induces long-lived immunity, but unlike natural infection, does not extract such a high price for immunity.

Of interest, a few vaccines induce a better immune response than natural infection:

- Human papillomavirus (HPV) vaccine—The high purity of the specific protein in the vaccine leads to a better immune reponse than natural infection.

- Tetanus vaccine—The toxin made by tetanus is so potent that the amount that causes disease is actually lower than the amount that induces a long-lasting immune response. This is why people with tetanus disease are still recommended to get the vaccine.

- *Haemophilus influenzae* type b (Hib) vaccine—children less than 2 years old do not typically make a good response to the complex sugar coating (polysaccharide) on the surface of Hib that causes disease; however, the vaccine links this polysaccharide to a helper protein that creates a better immune response than would occur naturally. Therefore, children less than 2 years old who get Hib are still recommended to get the vaccine.

- Pneumococcal vaccine—This vaccine works the same way as the Hib vaccine to create a better immune response than natural infection.

4

Evidence Does Not Show That Benefits of Vaccination Outweigh the Risks

Neil Z. Miller

Neil Z. Miller is a medical research journalist and the director of the Thinktwice Global Vaccine Institute.

Research on vaccine safety shows hazards and immunity limitations. Studies on vaccine safety are often exaggerated or false, and evidence of harm is often not reported by the mainstream media. Many studies are poorly designed, making it impossible to adequately assess the true safety of vaccines. In addition, there are often conflicts of interest in the way the studies are funded, calling into question the conclusions reached by researchers on vaccine safety.

I have been investigating vaccines for more than 25 years. When my son was born, the matter became important to me. I began by studying medical and scientific journals. The data was disturbing. Evidence showed that vaccines are often unsafe and ineffective. In fact, some vaccines cause new diseases. I was even more shocked to learn that powerful individuals within the organized medical profession—including members of the American Medical Association (AMA), the American Academy of Pediatrics (AAP), the Food and Drug Administration (FDA), the Centers for Disease Control and

Prevention (CDC), and the World Health Organization (WHO)—are aware of vaccine safety and protection deficiencies but seem to have an implicit agreement to obscure facts, alter truth, and deceive the public. Vaccine manufacturers, health officials, medical doctors, lead authors of important studies, editors of major medical journals, hospital personnel, and even coroners, cooperate to minimize vaccine failings, exaggerate benefits, and avert any negative publicity that might frighten concerned parents, threaten the vaccine program and lower vaccination rates.

Research on Vaccine Safety

During my research, I discovered a shadowy underworld of vaccine production and corruption within the industry. For example most people have no idea how vaccines are made or what they contain. Formaldehyde, aluminum and Thimerosal—yes, some vaccines still contain this dangerous mercury derivative arc just a few of the ingredients used to manufacture vaccines. In addition, oral polio vaccines are incubated in monkey kidneys, the chickenpox vaccine is brewed in "human embryonic lung cell cultures," and the new HPV vaccine includes particles of sexually transmitted viruses which are now being injected into an entire generation of chaste, young girls.

My main goal today in continuing to research vaccines is to provide families with evidence of vaccine safety and efficacy defects—information that they are unlikely to hear from their doctors—so that truly informed decisions can be made. Congressional efforts to initiate positive change within the vaccine industry have failed, so parents are the only remaining defense to protect their children. I am opposed to bogus "proofs" of vaccine benefits (including studies funded by vaccine manufacturers), health mandates (forced immunizations) and other coercive tactics used to intimidate wavering parents into vaccinating against their will. Although generations of children are falling victim to medical "progress," autism and other developmental disorders are *not* childhood rites of passage.

I researched vaccine studies and articles from around the world. There is extensive evidence of vaccine hazards and immunity limitations. I never intended to ratify traditional beliefs regarding vaccine safety and efficacy. Instead, my research is designed to countervail conventional dogma. The information I uncovered does not support the oft-heard claim that vaccine benefits outweigh their risks. If you'd like to read more about vaccine benefits and less about the risks, there are plenty of "official" websites that you can visit (or speak to your doctor). I encourage this course of action. Of course, official vaccine websites are mainly supported by vaccine manufacturers and allopathic health organizations such as the FDA, the CDC, and WHO—institutions with a mandate to promote vaccines and vaccinate as many people as possible.

---

80 percent of non-randomized studies turn out to be wrong, as do 25 percent of supposedly gold-standard randomized trials.

The Problem with Scientific Studies

Many "scientific" studies are literally nonsense. This is not a conspiracy theory. For example, the *Journal of the American Medical Association* recently published a paper [by John Ioannidis] showing that one-third of "highly cited original clinical research studies" were eventually contradicted by subsequent studies. The supposed effects of specific interventions either did not exist as the original studies concluded or were exaggerated.

PLOS Medicine recently published a paper entitled "Why Most Published Research Findings are False." The author of the study, Dr. John Ioannidis, is an internationally esteemed scientific researcher, epidemiologist, and Professor of Medicine at Stanford University. He concluded that "it is more likely for a research claim to be false than true." In fact, 80 percent of non-randomized studies turn out to be wrong, as do 25 percent of supposedly gold-standard randomized trials. "At every step in the process, there is room to distort results, a way to make a stronger claim or to select what is going to be concluded," says Ioannidis. Thus, vaccine studies need to be read very closely, otherwise significant information that could affect their validity may be overlooked.

In some instances, study results may be preordained. For example, when the vaccine-autism link became a public concern, vaccine proponents moved into high gear to produce authentic-appearing studies that contradicted genuine data. I remember when tobacco companies used this very same ploy. They financed numerous bogus studies ostensibly "proving" that cigarettes didn't cause cancer. The real studies got lost in the muddle. Sadly, it's all too easy to obfuscate truth and deceive the public.

Research That Shows Harm

At the infamous Simpsonwood conference held in Norcross, Georgia in June 2000, experts knew that Thimerosal (mercury) in vaccines was damaging children. They had irrefutable proof—the very reason for convening the meeting. (Dr. Tom Verstraeten, a CDC epidemiologist whose research was the focus of the meeting, had analyzed the agency's massive Vaccine Safety Datalink database containing thousands of medical records of vaccinated children. He declared: "We have found statistically significant relationships between exposure [to mercury in vaccines] and outcomes. At two months of age, developmental delay; exposure at three months, tics; at six months, attention deficit disorder. Exposures at one, three and six months, language and speech delays—the entire category of neurodevelopmental delays.")

Instead of making this important information public, authorities hatched a plan to produce additional "studies" that denied such a link. In fact, vaccine proponents had the audacity to claim in subsequent papers that mercury in vaccines not only doesn't hurt children but that it actually benefits them! In the topsy-turvy world of overreaching vaccine authorities, the well-documented neurotoxic chemical mercury somehow makes children smarter and more functional, *improving* cognitive development and motor skills. Of course, this is absurd. Many valid studies confirm mercury's destructive effect on brain development and behavior.

Sadly, the mainstream media rarely publishes anything that challenges the sacrosanct vaccine program.

Study conclusions often contradict core data in the study. I am always astounded when I read the abstract or summary of a major paper touting a vaccine's apparent safety or benefits, only to find that upon examining the actual paper, including important details, the vaccine is shown to be dangerous and may have poor efficacy as well. For example, a large study analyzed the safety of Thimerosal-containing vaccines (TCVs) and found dangerous side effects: "Cumulative exposure at 3 months resulted in a positive association with tics." In addition, there were "increased risks of language delay" for cumulative exposure at 3 months and 7 months. Yet, the paper [by T. Verstraeten et al.] concluded that "no consistent significant associations were found between TCVs and neurodevelopmental outcomes."

In another high profile study published in *JAMA Pediatrics* in January 2013, researchers [J.M. Glanz et al.] compared fully vaccinated children to children who were under-vaccinated due to parental choice. (These were parents who researched vaccines and decided not to follow the official immunization schedule.) The under-vaccinated children had "lower rates of outpatient visits and emergency department encounters." Yet, the paper concluded that "under-vaccinated children appear to have different healthcare utilization patterns." Sadly, the mainstream media rarely publishes anything that challenges the sacrosanct vaccine program. Newspaper stories about vaccines, and reviews of vaccine studies that are published, merely mimic the original spurious or deceptive conclusions.

Poorly Designed Studies

Another ploy used by vaccine proponents is to design studies comparing vaccinated people to other vaccinated people. Honest studies would compare vaccinated people to an *unvaccinated* population. For example, the clinical safety studies for the pneumococcal vaccine compared the number of adverse reactions in a group of infants who received the new shot, to a "control" group of infants who received a meningococcal vaccine and a DTaP shot. This created the illusion of a similar safety profile. The group receiving the new vaccine was never compared to a true control group of unvaccinated infants.

Vaccine control groups rarely receive a true placebo, which should be a harmless substance. The scientific method has always been predicated upon removing all potentially confounding influences. However, many vaccine studies do not conform to this integral component of valid research. This is an important concept to grasp. For example, when the HPV vaccine was tested for safety, one group of female teenagers was injected with the experimental HPV vaccine (which is manufactured with an aluminum adjuvant to stimulate antibodies) while the "control" group received an injection of aluminum as well (rather than a harmless substance).

When a new rotavirus vaccine was tested for safety, the "control" group received a placebo that "had the same constituents as the active vaccine but without the vaccine virus." Thus, the control group received a solution containing ferric (III) nitrate, magnesium sulfate, phenol red, and 10 additional chemical substances—everything that was in the experimental vaccine minus the rotavirus. When new vaccines are compared to other vaccines or to placebos that are not harmless, the rate of adverse reactions in the control group will be artificially high making the new vaccine appear safer than it really is. Whenever this deceptive tactic is utilized, the manufacturer may claim that its new vaccine has a "non-inferior" safety profile.

Some clinical studies that are used to license vaccines exclude people in certain groups. For example, they may be too young, too old, pregnant, ill, or have other preexisting health ailments. However, once the vaccine is licensed, it may be recommended for people in these groups. Much like using false placebos, this unethical practice artificially inflates the vaccine's safety profile and places more people at risk of adverse reactions. For example, the *New England Journal of Medicine* published a large study that looked at whether administering Thimerosal-containing vaccines to infants is safe. However, this study excluded infants from the study if their birth weight was less than 5.5 pounds—even though low birth weight infants are more likely to have serious reactions to Thimerosal-containing vaccines and low birth weight infants throughout society received them! (Vaccines are not adjusted for the weight of the child. Today, a 6-pound newborn receives the same dose of hepatitis B vaccine—with the same amount of aluminum and formaldehyde—as a 12-pound toddler.)

When important vaccine studies are jeopardized by conflicts of interest, generations of people—and society itself—are placed at risk.

In another study, 73 percent of all children that were hospitalized after being infected with chickenpox (varicella) were healthy before contracting the disease; just 27 percent had preexisting health problems. (A small number of children who contract varicella experience serious complications. Many of these children have preexisting health problems, such as AIDS, leukemia or cancer. However, it's easier to convince parents to vaccinate their children against a relatively benign disease such as chickenpox—and to justify mandating this shot for *all* children—if a larger percentage of those who experience complications of varicella are *healthy*, rather than *unhealthy*, before the onset of the ailment. This is because it's frightening to imagine that your normal child could be devastated by a common disease. Thus, after the chickenpox vaccine was licensed, several articles began to appear asserting that such complications occur "predominantly" in children in whom one would not predict problems.) However, one very important bit of information was easy to miss if you only skimmed the study—*it excluded oncology patients!* In other words, this "study" omitted *unhealthy* children (with cancer) from analysis, then claimed that serious complications mainly occurred in *healthy* boys and girls.

Conflicts of Interest

Vaccine studies may be funded by pharmaceutical companies that have a financial interest in the outcome. Lead authors of crucial studies that are used to validate the safety or efficacy of a vaccine are often beholden to the manufacturer in some way. They may own stock in the company or may be paid by the manufacturer to travel around the country promoting their vaccines. Lead authors may receive consultation fees, grants or other benefits from the drug maker. For example, the large pharmaceutical company that manufactured the shingles vaccine (Merck) participated in oversight activities and monitored the progress of the primary study that was used to justify licensing this vaccine. In addition, some leading authors of this study received consultation fees, lecture fees, and honoraria from Merck. Some study authors received grant support from Merck or owned stock in the company while concurrently working on the study, or had "partial interests in relevant patents."

Several of the authors of the main clinical study on the efficacy of the HPV vaccine—the FDA looks at this study to determine if this vaccine should be licensed—were either current or former employees of the HPV manufacturer. Some of the study authors had an equity interest or held stock options in this company. Several of the study authors received consulting fees from or served on paid advisory boards to this company. These practices contravene ethical boundaries and compromise the integrity of the study. When important vaccine studies are jeopardized by conflicts of interest, generations of people—and society itself—are placed at risk.

5

Evidence Shows Vaccines Unrelated to Autism

Immunization Action Coalition

The Immunization Action Coalition is a nonprofit organization that works to increase immunization rates by educating the public about the benefits of vaccines.

Despite worries about a connection between autism and vaccines, the evidence does not support a causal link between the two. The number of vaccines given and the additives in vaccines have all been proven to be safe, including the mercury-containing compound thimerosal. The rumors about a connection between the MMR (measles, mumps, and rubella) vaccine and autism were started by a British journal article that has since been retracted.

Claims that vaccines cause autism have led some parents to delay or refuse vaccines for their children. The most common claims are that autism is caused by measles-mumps-rubella (MMR) vaccine, vaccines that contain thimerosal, or too many vaccines. Many studies have been done to test these claims. None has shown that vaccines cause autism. The real causes of autism are not fully known, but scientists—working with families—have made progress.

This sheet lays out the facts to help parents understand why experts do not think vaccines cause autism.

Medical and Legal Authorities Agree That No Evidence Exists That Vaccines Cause Autism

The Institute of Medicine is an impartial group of the world's leading experts that advises Congress on science issues. After reviewing more than 200 studies in 2004 and more than 1,000 studies in 2011, the consensus report strongly stated that the evidence did not show a link between vaccines and autism.

In 2014, researchers from the RAND Corporation published an update to the 2011 Institute of Medicine's report. In a systematic review of the evidence published on vaccine safety to date, they found the evidence was strong that MMR vaccine is not associated with autism.

In 2009, the U.S. federal court reviewed 939 medical articles in their hearings. The court found the evidence was "overwhelmingly contrary" to the theory that autism is linked to MMR vaccine, thimerosal, or a combination of the two.

Based on the research, the World Health Organization, the European Medicines Agency, Health Canada, and other national and international health groups have concluded that no link can be found between vaccines and autism.

The Causes of Autism Are Not Fully Understood, but the Evidence Does Not Point Toward Vaccines

Parents often first notice the behaviors of autism when their child is 18–24 months old—the age by which most childhood vaccines have been given. Because of this, many parents incorrectly associate vaccination with the onset of autism. Developmental specialists, however, can identify early signs of autism in children when they are much younger, before their parents have noticed anything unusual. This research supports the scientific consensus that, in most cases, the precursors of autism are present before a child is born.

The influence of vaccines on a child cannot explain the measurable differences in brain structure and brain function that exist between autistic and non-autistic children. Starting in the first six months of life, many autistic children experience unusually rapid growth in areas of the brain that are responsible for the skills typically impaired in autism. Researchers have used "functional" MRI [magnetic resonance imaging] scans to study the connections in areas of the brain that control language, social and emotional processes, suggesting that these abnormalities contribute to the development of autism. The results of these and other studies provide promising clues for future research on the causes of autism and emphasize that finding its causes will not be as simple as pointing to vaccines as the cause.

From the moment of a baby's birth, the immune system begins coping with microorganisms in the form of bacteria, viruses, and fungi.

What is known with great certainty is that genetics play a major role in determining whether a child will be autistic. The study of twins bears this out. Identical twins have 100% of their genes in common; fraternal twins have 50% in common (like any other pair of siblings). In more than three out of four cases, when one identical twin has a form of autism, the other one does too. Among fraternal twins, though, this is true for one out of about seven pairs, at most. A child who has one or more older siblings with autism is between 20 and 50 times more likely to be diagnosed with a form of autism, compared with a child who has no autistic older siblings. In addition, in families affected by autism, many parents and non-autistic siblings display mild autistic-like traits. The inherited or spontaneous mutations that seem to be associated with autism are in genes that control the development of the brain—including how brain cells develop and make circuits that operate correctly. This finding agrees with the discovery of abnormalities in the way the brain operates even in very young infants and toddlers with autism.

Eric Courchesne and his colleagues at the University of California, San Diego, recently confirmed that the brains of children with autism have distinct patches of architectural disorganization in their prefrontal and temporal cortical tissue. Because the organization of the cortex begins in the second trimester of pregnancy, the researchers conclude that the events leading to the malformation of the cortex must begin around this time or earlier, certainly well before a child is born or ever receives a vaccine.

A Baby's Immune System Can Easily Handle the Vaccines Recommended for Infants and Toddlers

Some people worry that receiving too many vaccines early in life can overwhelm a baby's immune system and that this might somehow lead to autism. This doesn't fit with what we know about the remarkable capacity of the immune system. From the moment of a baby's birth, the immune system begins coping with microorganisms in the form of bacteria, viruses, and fungi. Like vaccines, these microorganisms contain foreign antigens—proteins that stimulate the immune system. When you realize that a single bacterium contains a larger variety and number of antigens than are found in all the recommended early childhood vaccines combined, you can see that a baby's immune system, which copes with exposure to countless bacteria each day, can easily withstand exposure to the antigens in vaccines.

No Links Between Autism and Thimerosal

A mercury-containing compound, thimerosal has been used since the 1930s as a vaccine preservative in vials that contain several doses of vaccine (called multi-dose vials). Before giving a vaccine, a health-care professional inserts the needle of the syringe that will be used to administer the vaccine into the stopper of the multi-dose vial and draws out a single dose of vaccine. When the needle pierces the stopper, it is possible that contaminants from outside the vial might be introduced, even when sterile technique is used. Thimerosal keeps bacteria or other microorganisms that might have entered the vaccine vial from multiplying.

Today, influenza vaccine is the only childhood vaccine licensed for use in the U.S. that contains more than a trace of thimerosal, and we know that it is safe for children.

Studies to determine if a relationship exists between thimerosal-containing vaccines and autism have taken two different approaches: (1) some examined groups of children who had received childhood vaccines that contained varying amounts of thimerosal. Autism occurred at essentially the same rate no matter how much or little thimerosal the children had received. (2) Other studies took the opposite approach, comparing autistic and non-autistic children to see if the autistic children had received more thimerosal-containing vaccines. No significant differences were found in the number of thimerosal-containing vaccines the two groups had received.

Why Was Thimerosal in Childhood Vaccines?

The mercury compound in thimerosal—ethylmercury—is chemically different from methylmercury, which is widely recognized as an environmental pollutant. Two key differences are that, unlike methylmercury, ethylmercury is (1) excreted from the body quickly, and (2) not easily transported across the blood-brain barrier (a structure of tightly packed cells that keeps potentially harmful substances in the bloodstream from entering the brain). The amount of ethylmercury in a thimerosal-preserved vaccine is minuscule compared with the amount of mercury that is required to cause symptoms of mercury poisoning. Also, the signs and symptoms of mercury poisoning are very different from the characteristics of autism. The chemical difference between ethylmercury and methylmercury is similar to the difference between ethyl alcohol, found in wine and beer, and methyl alcohol (wood alcohol), a poison found in antifreeze.

As a precaution, by 2001, all routinely recommended childhood vaccines were changed to single-dose packaging so they wouldn't require thimerosal. At the time, this was thought prudent, but all the evidence that has emerged since then shows that there was never a danger of children being harmed by thimerosal in vaccines. In 2004, the CDC [Centers for Disease Control and Prevention] began recommending influenza vaccine for all children 6 to 23 months old; some influenza vaccine formulations come in multi-dose vials that are preserved with thimerosal. Today, influenza vaccine is the only-childhood vaccine licensed for use in the U.S. that contains more than a trace of thimerosal, and we know that it is safe for children.

Studies Have Found No Link Between Autism and MMR Vaccine

Some studies of MMR vaccine compared groups of children who had received MMR vaccine against those who had not. These studies found that neither group was more likely to develop autism. Other studies looked at comparable groups of autistic and non-autistic children. These studies found that autistic children were no more likely to have received MMR vaccine.

Rumors about the safety of MMR vaccine first arose about a decade ago after a British physician (a gastroenterologist, not a person trained in either vaccinology or in neurological disorders) announced he had found virus from measles vaccines lingering in the intestines of 12 autistic children. He believed this accounted for their autism. Other researchers, however, were never able to replicate these results, which implied the gastroenterologist's conclusions were erroneous. Later, a press investigation revealed that the doctor had falsified patient data and relied on laboratory reports that he had been warned were incorrect. The journal that originally published his study took the unusual step of retracting it from the scientific literature on the grounds that it was the product of dishonest and irresponsible research, and British authorities revoked the doctor's license to practice medicine.

The fear that vaccines might cause autism is a dangerous myth. Much scientific research has been devoted to this topic. The result has been an ever-increasing and uniformly reassuring body of evidence that childhood vaccination is, in fact, entirely unrelated to the development of autism. The readings below may be of interest to parents who wish to learn more.

References

1. Immunization Action Coalition. Decisions in the Omnibus Autism Proceeding. www.immunize.org/catg.d/p4029.pdf

2. Institute of Medicine. *Adverse Effects of Vaccines: Evidence and Causality*. National Academies Press. 2011. www.iom.edu/Reports/2011/Adverse-Effects-of -Vaccines-Evidence-and-Causality.aspx

3. Institute of Medicine. *Immunization Safety Review: Vaccines and Autism*. National Academies Press. 2004. www.iom.edu/Reports/2004/Immunization-Safety -Review-Vaccines-and-Autism.aspx

4. Maglione MA, Das L, Raaen L, et al. Safety of Vaccines Used for Routine Immunization of U.S. Children: A Systematic Review. *Pediatrics*, published ahead of print July 1, 2014.

5. Autism Science Foundation. www.autismsciencefoundation.org

6. Centers for Disease Control and Prevention (CDC), National Center for Birth Defects and Developmental Disabilities. Autism Spectrum Disorders. www.cdc .gov/ncbddd/autism/facts.html

7. National Institutes of Health. National Institute of Child Health and Development: Autism Spectrum Disorder (ASD): NICHD Research Information. www.nichd.nih.gov/health/topics/autism/researchinfo/Pages/default.aspx

8. Offit PA, Quarles J, Gerber MA, et al. Addressing parents' concerns: do multiple vaccines overwhelm or weaken the infant's immune system? *Pediatrics.* 2002;109(1):124–129. http://pediatrics.aappublications.org/cgi/content/abstract/109/1/124

9. Vaccine Education Center, Children's Hospital of Philadelphia. Too Many Vaccines? What You Should Know. Available at www.chop.edu/export/download/pdfs/articles/vaccine-education-center/too-many-vaccines.pdf

10. American Academy of Pediatrics. Vaccine Safety: Examine the Evidence. http://www2.aap.org/immunization/families/faq/VaccineStudies.pdf

11. Pichichero ME, Gentile A, Giglio N, et al., Mercury levels in newborns and infants after receipt of thimerosal-containing vaccines. *Pediatrics.* 2008; 121(2):e208–214. http://pediatrics.aappublications.org/cgi/content/full/121/2/e208

12. Nelson KB, Bauman ML. Thimerosal and autism? *Pediatrics.* 2003;111(3):674–679. http://pediatrics.aappublications.org/cgi/content/full/111/3/674

13. CDC. Notice to Readers: Thimerosal in Vaccines: A joint statement of the American Academy of Pediatrics and the Public Health Service. MMWR. 1999;48(26):563–565. www.cdc.gov/mmwr/preview/mmwrhtml/mm4826a3.htm

14. US Food and Drug Administration. www.fda.gov/BiologicsBloodVaccines/SafetyAvailability/VaccineSafety/UCM096228

15. Immunization Action Coalition. MMR Vaccine Does Not Cause Autism. www.immunize.org/catg.d/p4026.pdf

16. Offit PA. *Autism's False Prophets: Bad Science, Risky Medicine, and the Search for a Cure.* New York: Columbia University Press; 2008.

6

The Anti-Vaccine Movement Endangers the Disabled

David M. Perry

David M. Perry is an associate professor of history at Dominican University in Illinois.

The anti-vaccine movement is especially dangerous when it uses celebrities to promote its agenda. Parents of disabled children have reason to want to believe in possible causes and cures— even if it's clearly fraudulent—and the anti-vaccine movement has been successful at gaining followers. The movement has led to a breakdown in important herd immunity, as well as shifting attention and resources away from other issues, such as the need to include disabled children in society.

Last week [July 3, 2013], the state Supreme Court of Wisconsin upheld the reckless homicide convictions of Dale and Leilani Neumann. Their daughter, Madeline, had diabetes, a 99.8 percent treatable condition. When she grew sick, her parents decided to pray for her instead of taking her to a doctor. The parents belonged to no specific denomination forbidding medical treatment, but had started to correspond with a controversial Florida apocalyptic ministry that advocates faith healing. As they prayed, the child died.

The Neumann case provides a stark reminder that some beliefs can literally endanger children's lives. Religion and science equally fuel this kind of fear-mongering and reckless parenting. When combined with celebrity, real people get hurt.

A Celebrity Anti-Vaccinator

This week, news leaked that *The View*, a popular daytime talk show featuring a panel of four women, is considering making [actress] Jenny McCarthy one of their hosts. This is a mistake, as it would provide a platform for a dangerous voice. Over the last decade, McCarthy has become one of the most prominent voices against vaccinations. She declared, as a fact, that vaccinations had caused her son's autism, and promoted this idea in venues aimed at mothers, such as on *Oprah* [*Winfrey Show*].

McCarthy later insisted that she had cured their son through a combination of diet and vitamins. She accuses the government of being afraid to confront "the truth" about vaccines. In the last year or so, although she now admits her son never had autism, she is still selling fear by talking about the schedule of vaccines as dangerous. She has put the full force of her celebrity to the task of convincing parents to leave their children vulnerable.

It's happening right now, as diseases long rendered un-threatening are roaring back into dangerous life.

McCarthy makes the most sense viewed not through her celebrity lens, but as a fairly typical parent of a child facing a diagnosis of special needs. My son also has special needs, in his case Down syndrome, and I can tell you that the moment of diagnosis is hard and the days and months that follow are even harder. As I oscillated between hope and fear and tried to come to an understanding of my new life, I too looked for something to blame. Those powerful words, "Down syndrome," instantly transformed my life and the life of my family. I mourned for the loss of my idea of a "normal" son. Is it any wonder that McCarthy, having encountered the future laden with the word "autism," believed the myth of the vaccine and the hope for a cure? Is it any wonder that so many other parents have seized on this fraudulent accusation and related false hopes? I empathize with McCarthy, but that doesn't erase the real harm she has done.

The Importance of Herd Immunity

Anti-vaccinators risk not only the lives of their own children, but also those of others who are too medically fragile to get vaccinated and must instead rely on "herd immunity." Many medical conditions, especially those which compromise the immune system (which is fairly common in the world of Down syndrome), make vaccines medically inappropriate. Happily, in a population of vaccinated people, infectious but preventable diseases have trouble spreading even to the immunocompromised. But herd immunity breaks down when vaccinations are not administered to all who can medically receive them. At that point, people who chose to refuse vaccinations endanger those who had no choice.

It's happening right now, as diseases long rendered unthreatening are roaring back into dangerous life. We've seen a rapid increase of outbreaks in preventable diseases, such as pertussis (whooping cough), measles, and mumps in the U.S. and the U.K. [United Kingdom]. Whooping cough, for example, hit its highest rate of infection in 50 years over the last winter in the United States. A website dedicated to tracking the illnesses and deaths associated with the anti-vaccine movement cites over 100,000 illnesses and over 1,000 deaths from these preventable diseases.

McCarthy joined this dangerous movement after her son turned two and began to experience seizures and speech delays. He was diagnosed with autism, and she seized on research out of England that linked vaccinations to autism. That research was fraudulent. In 1998, Andrew Wakefield, who had a financial stake in an alternative MMR (Measles-Mumps-Rubella) vaccine, published a study in *The Lancet* that argued for a causal link between the traditional MMR vaccine and autism. His study was a corrupt version of a "case-control" trial, a notoriously unreliable format, based on just 12 children with autism. Such a tiny trial, even if perfectly conducted (and it was not), could tell very little about the wider population. Multiple larger trials refuted Wakefield's conclusion; moreover, Wakefield was found to have manipulated the evidence. Wakefield was stripped of his license to practice medicine and *The Lancet* took the extraordinary step of retracting the article. For Wakefield and his backers, like McCarthy, it's all a sign of a conspiracy.

People with autism are not victims, and they do not need McCarthy's organization to "rescue" them.

Meanwhile, children are literally getting sick and dying. By 2009, just when McCarthy's anti-vaccine message was reaching a peak, one study in Oregon found parents four-times as likely to skip vaccines as they had been four years before. Despite a CDC [Centers for Disease Control and Prevention] study of over 1,000 children showing no links between autism and vaccines (remember, Wakefield had only 12), parents keep asking about the risks of autism. And the specific MMR-related fears about autism has bled into more generalized fears about vaccination, as witnessed in the debate over the HPV [human papillomavirus] vaccine. All the evidence points to the HPV vaccine as one of the greatest and safest developments in recent medical history, but parents are afraid to take a step which would protect their children against life-threatening cancers.

The Needs of the Disabled

Beyond these generalized health issues, and here I am writing from the perspective of a parent deeply involved in the disability community, the notion that it is worth the risk of serious or even fatal illness to avoid autism hurts people who are living with the condition. McCarthy portrays autism as a terrifying disease you can nevertheless fix with fad diets. Claims of cures like McCarthy's have led parents to feed their children bleach, buy expensive (though harmless) specialized diets, and spend tens of thousands of dollars on experimental treatments.

People with autism need support in their quest for self-advocacy and integration, not fads. Parents need communities and schools and scientifically-guided medical care that they can rely on, not to be bilked by fraudsters and fearmongers. People with autism are not victims, and they do not need McCarthy's organization to "rescue" them. What they need is the same thing all persons with disability need: a pathway to inclusion.

I don't watch *The View*, but I do watch the world of disability, and I know the price that we pay when dangerous conspiracy theories spread. People in general, and parents in particular, are bad at assessing risks. We fear anthrax more than flu, sharks more than pigs, flying more than driving, terrorism more than handguns, and autism more than measles. We also believe in celebrity, something that McCarthy acknowledges when she says, "It is amazing what celebrity can do if you do it with 100 percent good intention and heart." I believe her intentions are good. As parents, we want the best for our children, and for all children with special needs. But in her case, the results have been terrible.

7

Parents Who Don't Vaccinate Children Make Us Sick

Amity Shlaes

Amity Shlaes is a columnist for Forbes *and director of the Four Percent Growth Project at the Bush Center.*

Increasing numbers of parents are foregoing vaccinations for their children, endangering others. The parents who choose to skip vaccinations are generally wealthier, and the anti-vaccine movement has led to several areas of the country where dangerously high percentages of children are unvaccinated. The result has been a resurgence of diseases not only for unvaccinated children but also for children with compromised immune systems and for babies too young to be immunized.

Young parents in America are holy and not to be messed with. If they say something is correct, we all acquiesce. And is there any man, woman or canine who doesn't leap out of the way when one of those giant, all-terrain Bugaboo strollers comes barreling down the sidewalk?

The impulse to butt out of parents' business is natural. Our culture hardwires us to respect those who are rearing children. We gave them a job to do, so we should let them do it.

Yet there's one smug subgroup whose sense of entitlement endangers the rest. No, not poor Medicaid moms or Social Security grannies. The treacherous group is those parents, predominately those of some financial means, who refuse to vaccinate their children.

Anxiety about vaccinations starts with a legitimate concern: the medicine can cause allergic reactions. General worry became specific controversy in 1998, when *The Lancet*, a respected medical journal, published a paper by U.K. [United Kingdom] physician Andrew Wakefield and others saying that the standard vaccine for measles, mumps and rubella might cause autism.

Later studies couldn't confirm Wakefield's findings, and the *Lancet* retracted the paper in 2010.

Yet many parents still won't vaccinate their kids. Some people in the U.S. have made an avocation of trying to secure a so-called personal belief waiver to allow their children to attend school without vaccines. Parents of autistic youngsters turned to the courts to blame drugmakers.

No-Fault Alternative

Fortunately, the anti-vaccine crowd's ability to create public-health problems was limited by the federal government's National Vaccine Injury Compensation Program. It compensates those injured by certain vaccines while discouraging large class-action lawsuits. This, in turn, frees drug companies to concentrate on new vaccines for illnesses such as cervical cancer.

Still, skipping these preventive steps has become trendy. Former U.K. Prime Minister Tony Blair and his wife, Cherie, fanned the fires by coyly refusing to say whether their youngest child was being vaccinated on the usual schedule. Actress Jenny McCarthy has done her part to inspire the no-vaccine movement with an ad campaign.

Paul Offit, a physician and vaccine expert who is author of *Deadly Choices: How the Anti-Vaccine Movement Threatens Us All*, noted that in recent years there have been "whole school classes where no child is properly vaccinated."

Sick in California

In Marin County, California, officials recently reported that 7 percent of children in kindergarten there had vaccine waivers, compared with 1 percent elsewhere. Nationwide, it turns out that poor parents are more sensible. Paul Howard and James R. Copland, scholars at the Manhattan Institute, report that 91.2 percent of Medicaid children receive the measles-mumps rubella vaccine compared with 90.6 percent of children in private health plans.

The sad results are already in.

The anti-vaccine crowd, short of evidence, has reverted to personal attack.

An unvaccinated boy from New York contracted mumps while in the U.K., then traveled home and attended summer camp. Within six months, hundreds of cases of mumps were counted, including some that led to pancreatitis, deafness and meningitis, Offit wrote. A child in Minnesota died of Haemophilus B influenza after his parents opposed vaccinations. In January 2008, an unvaccinated child flew home to San Diego following a trip to Switzerland, and gave the gift of measles to dozens of others, including three children in a doctor's waiting room.

Personal Attacks

Marin County, known for the fitness of its citizens, endured 15 percent of California's whooping cough cases in 2010, even though it accounts for less than 1 percent of the state's population. Ten children died, none of whom had been vaccinated, Offit told me in a phone call.

The anti-vaccine crowd, short of evidence, has reverted to personal attack. It argues, for example, that Offit is beholden to the pharmaceutical business, having developed RotaTeq, a vaccine sold by Merck to fight a common cause of childhood vomiting and diarrhea. But Offit said in an e-mail that he receives no royalties from RotaTeq sales. The character assassination is taking place to obscure the strength of the case Offit makes.

Non-vaccinators aren't merely endangering their own children, or even other children whose parents oppose vaccination. All newborns must wait several months to be old enough for vaccinations. Vaccines are often too risky for people with compromised immune systems, regardless of age. It's newborns and chemotherapy patients, already physically vulnerable, who pay the price for parental NIMBYism [NIMBY stands for "Not In My Back Yard"].

Supreme Court Case

You can make a creepy Darwinist argument that this problem is self-correcting. In chastened California, that's already happening. Last fall then-Governor Arnold Schwarzenegger signed a law requiring junior and senior high school students to receive a vaccine for pertussis, or whooping cough, a highly contagious bacterial disease.

There is no self-correcting dynamic when it comes to diseases for which there isn't yet a vaccine. Within a few months the Supreme Court will decide whether the federal government's no-fault vaccine-compensation program can preempt all vaccine-defect claims. If the court says the program doesn't have that power, drug companies may become less interested in developing new vaccines.

That might dash hopes for a new cholera vaccine, much hoped-for in Africa, and also an innovation the entire globe longs for: a vaccine against sanctimony.

8

The Anti-Vaccine Movement Is Given False Equivalence by the Media

Katrina vanden Heuvel

Katrina vanden Heuvel is editor and publisher of The Nation.

The media attention given to the anti-vaccination views of actress Jenny McCarthy is dangerous. The view that vaccines and mercury cause autism has been thoroughly discredited by science. Airing McCarthy's view alongside that of doctors and scientists who support the safety and efficacy of vaccines gives a false sense of equivalence to these competing views—when in reality only one side is conveying the truth.

On February 28, 1998, a British physician named Andrew Wakefield published a paper in *The Lancet* that purported to identify a link between the measles, mumps and rubella (MMR) vaccine and the appearance of autism in children. The results provoked a widespread backlash against vaccines, forcing the medical community to spend years attempting to debunk his false claims. Eventually, it was revealed that Wakefield had fabricated his research as part of a scheme that promised him millions of dollars. Wakefield suffered a dramatic public downfall—his medical license stripped, his

Katrina vanden Heuvel, "Jenny McCarthy's Vaccination Fear-Mongering and the Cult of False Equivalence," *Nation*, July 22, 2013. Copyright © 2013 by Nation. Reprinted with permission from the July 12, 2013 issue of The Nation. For subscription information, call 1-800-333-8536. Portions of each week's Nation magazine can be accessed at http://www.thenation.com.

paper retracted from publication—but the damage was done. His propaganda had led to decreased immunization rates and an outbreak of measles in London [United Kingdom].

The Promotion of a Falsehood

Wakefield's falsified claims remain at the core of a stubbornly popular anti-vaccination movement. To this day, despite overwhelming evidence to the contrary, many people believe that vaccines are the principal cause of autistic spectrum disorders.

One of the most prominent promoters of this falsehood is actress Jenny McCarthy, who was recently named as Elisabeth Hasselbeck's replacement on ABC's hit daytime talk-show, *The View*. Once she's on air, it will be difficult to prevent her from advocating for the anti-vaccine movement. And the mere act of hiring her would seem to credit her as a reliable source.

In 2007, McCarthy debuted her views on the national stage when she appeared on *The Oprah Winfrey Show* to discuss autism, which is growing at alarming rates and continues to baffle medical researchers. McCarthy was convinced that vaccines gave her son autism and seizures. In addition to a gluten-free diet, aromatherapies, B-12 shots and vitamins, she also tried chelation therapy, which is meant to remove toxic substances from the body. Her son, she claimed, was "cured."

Within the first few minutes of the interview, McCarthy cited as reasons for her success a "little voice" and her "mommy instincts," all while denigrating several doctors and EMTs [emergency medical technicians].

Let's be clear: there is no connection between vaccines and autism.

The Airing of Disproven Ideas

Oprah Winfrey's decision to let McCarthy act as an expert, to dismiss science with alchemy, without asking any tough questions, was unconscionable. The same could be said of the producers of *Larry King Live* and *Good Morning America*, both of which hosted McCarthy soon after. Even though they at least asked questions about her views, Larry King had her debate a doctor, as though her disproven ideas should be given the same equivalence as those of a medical expert.

In fact, McCarthy's beliefs—that vaccines and mercury cause autism, that a good diet cures autism and that "diagnosticians and pediatricians have made a career out of telling parents autism is a hopeless condition"—have been roundly dismissed and discredited by doctors and scientists, who insist that her claims are based on no scientific data or research. McCarthy wasn't deterred. "The University of Google," she said to Oprah, "is where I got my degree from."

Let's be clear: there is no connection between vaccines and autism.

Despite the evidence, it is easy to understand why the parent of an autistic child—in fear and confusion and desperation—might find McCarthy's claims enticing. These are parents at their most vulnerable and McCarthy, though perhaps well intentioned, has preyed on them. This fear-mongering is incredibly dangerous, especially when a quarter of parents trust the information provided by celebrities about the safety of vaccines. A movement borne out of Wakefield's discredited research, animated by misinformation, and promoted by people like McCarthy has fed an anti-vaccine frenzy, leading to a huge spike in cases of whooping cough in communities across the United States, especially in Washington State, which, in 2012, saw its worst epidemic in seventy years.

We see the same dangerous nonsense playing out with the HPV [human papillomavirus] vaccine, a major breakthrough that can prevent cervical cancer and, it was recently found, throat cancer in men and women. Unfortunately, parents studying at McCarthy's alma mater, the University of Google, are absorbing misinformation and refusing to vaccinate their kids.

The Danger of False Equivalence in the Media

These incidents reflect a broader disconnect between science and the media on a range of issues. The vast majority of scientists accept that evolution is real, that man-made climate change is occurring and that vaccines do not cause autism. But in the general public, these issues are often hotly debated, and, too often, the media fuels these arguments by airing junk science as though it were legitimate. The result? A major public health risk. Vaccine avoidance makes the entire country more susceptible to diseases like the measles that were once vanquished.

By giving science deniers a public forum, media outlets implicitly condone their claims as legitimate. As *Columbia Journalism Review*'s Brendan Nyhan recently argued in a post about McCarthy and her vaccination fear-mongering, "he said" "she said" coverage simply puts "unsupported claims alongside credible arguments, or failed to push back altogether." False equivalency is one of journalism's great pitfalls, and in an effort to achieve "balance," reporters often obscure the truth. What's the merit in "he said, she said" reporting when he says the world is round and she insists it is flat. Indeed, there is an enormous cost to society when the truth could save lives.

9

State Vaccination Requirements Usually Allow Exemptions

Ben Kleifgen and Justin Silpe

Ben Kleifgen is a medical resident at the department of pediatrics at the University of Arizona College of Medicine. Justin Silpe is a researcher in internal medicine, chemistry, and biophysics at the University of Michigan.

The requirement to vaccinate children varies from state to state, but all states require children to receive certain vaccines to attend public school or state-licensed day care centers. All states have exemptions to these requirements for medical reasons, most states have exemptions for religious reasons, and almost half provide exemptions for philosophical reasons. The rate of nonmedical exemptions has increased in recent years with corresponding higher rates of disease.

Vaccination is one of a small group of medical interventions with direct benefits to *both* individuals and communities. When a large percentage of a population is vaccinated against a pathogen, the entire community—both those vaccinated and unvaccinated—receive additional protection. This concept, known as 'herd immunity,' is a primary justification for mandatory vaccination policies in the United States.

Vaccine Requirements in the United States

In the U.S., all states require children attending public school or state-licensed day care facilities to receive a series of vaccinations. Specific requirements vary from state to state. (Some states specifically include private schools in these requirements, while most private schools voluntarily adopt similar, if not identical, requirements for their students.) The term "mandate" is somewhat misleading when applied to vaccination, however. The last time the U.S. required vaccination without exception—a true mandate—was during World War I. Today, all states except Mississippi and West Virginia have procedures which allow parents to exempt their children from state vaccination requirements on the basis of religious and/or personal beliefs.

Vaccination requirements for school and day care attendance are seen as critical to ensuring high rates of vaccination in the U.S. Public health officials cite a number of reasons for this belief. Linking vaccination with school attendance, itself required by law, ensures that vaccines reach the greatest number of children. Schools are a prime venue for the transmission of vaccine-preventable disease, and active school-age children can further spread disease to their families and others with whom they interact.

State governments are solely responsible for school vaccination requirements.

An additional benefit of vaccination requirements is its ability to address disparities in vaccination rates. In a 2008 study published in *Pediatrics*, a hepatitis B vaccination requirement was found to improve large racial and ethnic disparities in vaccination rates seen prior to the introduction of the mandate.

While school vaccination requirements have contributed to significant decreases in the incidence of many vaccine-preventable diseases, opposition to these policies is increasingly prevalent. Such resistance is neither new nor unique to the United States, however. In fact, the term "conscientious objector" originally referred to opponents of England's aggressively-enforced smallpox vaccination requirement in the late nineteenth century.

State Law on School-Entry Vaccine Requirements

State governments are solely responsible for school vaccination requirements. The federal government has no role in recommending, approving, or enforcing policies that mandate vaccination for school or day-care attendance. Through the Department of Health and Human Services and its agencies— particularly the Food and Drug Administration (FDA) and Centers for Disease Control and Prevention (CDC)—the federal government licenses new vaccines for use in the U.S., provides recommendations on populations for whom specific vaccines should be administered, finances vaccines for uninsured or underinsured children, monitors vaccine safety, and promotes vaccination nationwide. However, the decision to add a vaccine to a state's required vaccination schedule is made only by state public health officials or state legislatures. In some states, adding a vaccine requirement can occur through regulations issued by its health department; others require a bill to be passed by the legislature and signed by the governor.

As noted previously, all 50 U.S. states and Washington, DC have school-entry requirements for vaccines. 48 allow exemptions for religious reasons (West Virginia and Mississippi are the only exceptions) and 21 allow for philosophical (also known as personal-belief) exemptions. All states also permit exemptions for medical reasons, such as children with weakened immune systems or allergic to a vaccine component. Home-schooled [children] are generally not subject to state vaccination requirements, making this option attractive to parents who wish neither to vaccinate their children nor to seek an exemption. As of 2010, only North Carolina requires vaccination of home-schooled children.

Children who have not received all required vaccinations or a valid exemption are not permitted to attend school, although enforcement varies widely among states. In the event of an outbreak, children with exemptions can be excluded from school attendance.

The Difference Between Religious and Philosophical Exemptions

The distinction between a philosophical (personal-belief) and a religious exemption is often ambiguous. The precise language varies from state to state, but for religious exemptions, states have required religious objections to be based on tenets of a specific, organized religion. Laws phrased in this way have been successfully challenged as violating Constitutional protections regarding the free exercise of religion, however. As a result, many states speak in far more general terms, such as "a sincere and meaningful belief . . . held with the strength of traditional religious convictions."

Communities with lower rates of immunization had higher rates of infection among vaccinated children *than those with higher vaccination rates.*

Parents who refuse vaccination on philosophical grounds point not to religious beliefs but often cite their right to determine the medical care of their children without government involvement. However, the U.S. Supreme Court has ruled on several occasions that state vaccination requirements are permissible, writing that "the very concept of ordered liberty precludes allowing every person to make his own standards on matters of conduct in which the society as a whole has important interests."

The Impact of Exemptions

An individual's decision to refuse vaccination can have societal consequences. In a community where vaccination rates are very high, the likelihood of members being exposed to a pathogen is quite low. As a result, it may actually be in any one individual's best interest *not* to get vaccinated, since they already benefit from a reduced likelihood of infection (due to high vaccination rates) without exposing themselves to any vaccine-associated risks, however small. An individual refusing vaccination by this logic could be termed a "free rider." However, if too many individuals adopt this approach, the additional benefits of herd immunity will be lost, and, since no vaccine is 100% effective, even those vaccinated will be at an increased risk. Recent outbreaks of vaccine-preventable diseases among the unvaccinated suggest that relying solely on herd immunity for personal protection is a dubious strategy, at best.

From 1991 to 2004, the average rate of non-medical exemptions from immunization requirements increased from .98 to 1.48%. Similar increases in non-medical exemptions have been observed during the past several years. This rate varies widely among states and even within particular regions thereof. Rates are especially high in states with personal-belief exemptions and those with particularly easy processes to obtain an exemption.

Two studies published in the *Journal of the American Medical Association* found that children exempt from vaccination requirements were more than 35 times more likely to contract measles and nearly 6 times more likely to contract pertussis, compared to vaccinated children. This research also showed that communities with lower rates of immunization had higher rates of infection *among vaccinated children* than those with higher vaccination rates. Similar correlations between exemption rates and incidence of vaccine-preventable disease has been found in both the United Kingdom and Japan.

10

People Should Not Be Allowed to Refuse Vaccination

Ronald Bailey

Ronald Bailey is the science correspondent for Reason *magazine and Reason.com, where he writes a weekly science and technology column.*

If the decision to refuse vaccination only affected the individual, then refusal would be permissible, but refusing vaccination puts others in harm's way. Vaccines have decreased the mortality and suffering caused by infectious diseases. People who refuse to vaccinate take advantage of the large majority of people who do vaccinate, free-riding off of their immunity. As more people refuse vaccination, herd immunity starts to fail and this puts everyone at risk.

A significant proportion of Americans believe it is perfectly all right to put other people at risk of the costs and misery of preventable infectious diseases. These people are your friends, neighbors, and fellow citizens who refuse to have themselves or their children vaccinated against contagious diseases.

There would be no argument against allowing people to refuse vaccination if they and their families would suffer alone the consequences of their foolhardiness. It would be their right to forego misery-reducing and life-preserving treatments. But that is not the case in the real world.

Ronald Bailey, "Refusing Vaccination Puts Others at Risk: A Pragmatic Argument for Coercive Vaccination," Reason.com, December 6, 2013. Copyright © 2013 by Reason Foundation. All rights reserved. Reproduced by permission.

A Decline in Infectious Disease Mortality

The University of Pittsburgh's Project Tycho database, launched last week [November 28, 2013], quantifies the prevalence of infectious disease since 1888 in the United States. Drawing on Project Tycho data, a November 28 *New England Journal of Medicine [NEJM]* article concluded that vaccinations since 1924 until now prevented 103 million cases of polio, measles, rubella, mumps, hepatitis A, diphtheria, and pertussis. While the *NEJM* article did not calculate the number of deaths avoided as a result of vaccination, one of the study's authors estimates that number is between three and four million.

The risk that infectious diseases will kill innocent bystanders is not the only issue. Sheer misery counts too.

People who don't wish to take responsibility for their contagious microbes will often try to justify their position by noting the fact that the mortality rates of many infectious diseases had declined significantly before vaccines came along. And it is certainly true that a lot of that decline in infectious disease mortality occurred as a result of improved sanitation and water chlorination. A 2004 study by the Harvard University economist David Cutler and the National Bureau of Economic Research economist Grant Miller estimated that the provision of clean water "was responsible for nearly half of the total mortality reduction in major cities, three-quarters of the infant mortality reduction, and nearly two-thirds of the child mortality reduction." Improved nutrition also reduced mortality rates, enabling infants, children, and adults to fight off diseases that would have more likely killed their malnourished ancestors.

But vaccines have played a substantial role in reducing death rates too. An article in the *Journal of the American Medical Association* compared the annual average number of cases and resulting deaths of various diseases before the advent of vaccines to those occurring in 2006. Before an effective diphtheria vaccine was developed, for example, there were about 21,000 cases of the disease each year, 1,800 of them leading to death. No cases or deaths from the disease were recorded in 2006. Measles averaged 530,000 cases and 440 deaths per year before the vaccine. In 2006, there were 55 cases and no deaths. Whooping cough saw around 200,000 cases and 4,000 deaths annually. In 2006, there were nearly 16,000 cases and 27 deaths. Polio once averaged around 16,000 cases and 1,900 deaths. No cases were recorded in 2006. The number of Rubella cases dropped from 48,000 to 17, and the number of deaths dropped from 17 to zero.

With the latter disease, the more important measure is the number of babies, born to rubella-infected mothers, who suffered from disease-induced birth defects, such as deafness, cloudy corneas, damaged hearts, and stunted intellects. Some 2,160 infants were afflicted with congenital rubella syndrome as late as 1965. In 2006 it was one.

The Impact of Infectious Diseases

The risk that infectious diseases will kill innocent bystanders is not the only issue. Sheer misery counts too. The fevers, the sweats, the incessant coughs, the runny noses, the itchy rashes, and the lost days at work must be taken into account, too. And, of course, many people end up in the hospital as a result of infectious disease.

Before a chicken pox vaccine became available, upwards of four million kids got the disease every year, of which 11,000 were hospitalized and 105 died. In 2004, the estimated number of cases had dropped to 600,000, resulting in 1,276 hospitalizations and 19 deaths. Before the measles vaccine was introduced in 1962, some 48,000 were hospitalized and 450 died of that infection each year. So far this year [2013] there have been 175 cases and three hospitalizations. A 1985 study by

Centers for Disease Control and Prevention epidemiologist in the journal *Pediatrics* estimated that the first 20 years of measles vaccination in the U.S. had prevented 52 million cases, 5,200 deaths and 17,400 cases of mental retardation.

In rich countries, few children die of rotavirus diarrheal disease, but it does kill some 500,000 kids living in poor countries annually. Prior to 2006, when vaccines against rotavirus became available, about one in five kids under the age of five in the United States annually came down with it, of which 57,000 were hospitalized. Subsequent to widespread vaccination, hospitalization rates have dropped by 90 percent. Interestingly, rotavirus hospitalizations among older children and young adults who are not immunized have also fallen by around 10,000 annually. Why? Because they are no longer exposed to the disease by infants who would otherwise have infected them.

Whooping cough incidence rates have been increasing along with the number of people refusing immunization for their kids.

The Harm of Free-Riding

Vaccines do not produce immunity in some people, so a percentage of those who took the responsibility to be vaccinated remain vulnerable. This brings us to the important issue of herd immunity. Herd immunity works when most people are immunized against an illness, greatly reducing the chances that an infected person can pass his microbes along to other susceptible people, such as infants who cannot yet be vaccinated, immunocompromised individuals, or folks who have refused the protection of vaccination.

People who refuse vaccination for themselves and their children are free-riding off herd immunity. Anti-vaccination folks are taking advantage of the fact that most people around them have chosen the minimal risk of vaccination, thus acting as a firewall protecting them from disease. But if enough refuse, the firewall comes down and other people get hurt.

Oliver Wendell Holmes articulated a good libertarian principle when he said, "The right to swing my fist ends where the other man's nose begins." Holmes' observation is particularly salient in the case of whooping cough shots.

Infants cannot be vaccinated against whooping cough, so their protection against this dangerous disease depends upon the fact that most of the rest of us are immunized against it. Unfortunately, whooping cough incidence rates have been increasing along with the number of people refusing immunization for their kids. The annual number of pertussis cases fell to a low of 1,010 in 1976. Last year, the number of reported cases rose to 48,277, the highest number since 1955. Eighteen infants died of the disease in 2012, and half of the infants who got it were hospitalized.

In 2005, an intentionally unvaccinated 17-year-old girl brought measles back with her from a visit to Romania and ended up infecting 34 people. Most of them were also intentionally unvaccinated, but a medical technician who had been vaccinated caught the disease as well and was hospitalized. Despite the medical technician's bad luck, the good news is that the measles vaccine is thought to protect 99.8 percent of [those] who get the shot. Similarly, in 2008 an intentionally unvaccinated seven-year-old boy sparked an outbreak of measles in San Diego. The boy, who caught the disease in Switzerland, ended up spreading his illness to 11 other children, all of whom were also unvaccinated, putting one infant in the hospital. Forty-eight other kids who were too young to be vaccinated were quarantined.

To borrow Holmes' metaphor, people who refuse vaccination are asserting that they have a right to "swing" their microbes at other people. There is no principled libertarian case for their free-riding refusal to take responsibility for their own microbes.

11

Should You Get the HPV Vaccine?

Jake Blumgart

Jake Blumgart is a reporter, researcher, and editor.

Vaccines for the sexually transmitted human papillomavirus (HPV) help prevent numerous cancers linked to HPV. Although HPV has been seen in the past as a women's health issue because of its link with cervical cancer, more types of cancers linked with HPV are on the rise, including some that affect men. Although it is best to get vaccinated from HPV when one is young, prior to becoming sexually active, there are scenarios where an older person should consider the vaccine.

The human papillomavirus [HPV] has the dubious distinction of being the sexually transmitted disease you are most likely to get. It's also the leading cause of cervical cancer. January has, somewhat arbitrarily, been dubbed Cervical Health Awareness Month (also National Hobby Month and Hot Tea Month, the last at least for good reason). While cervical cancer is the disease most commonly associated with HPV, a recent report from the American Cancer Society emphasizes that HPV's threat is not gender-specific or organ-specific. While cervical cancer cases are in decline (as are general cancer rates), cancers linked to HPV are on the rise.

The Rise in HPV-Linked Cancers

The increasing prevalence of HPV-linked cancers should permanently alter our limited conception of the disease as chiefly a women's issue. Oropharyngeal (which I'll be vulgarizing as "oral") and anal HPV-related cancers (which particularly afflict men who have sex with men) are becoming more common. Oral malignancies account for 37.3 percent of HPV-related cancers, edging out cervical cancer, which makes up 32.7 percent. For men, oral cancers make up 78.2 percent of total HPV-related cancer incidences, and they account for 11.6 percent of cases among women. The death rate for oral cancer is three times higher than that for cervical cancer. (About 40 percent of penile cancer cases are HPV-related, but rates of the disease have basically remained static.)

More data and publicity for the vaccines could improve the vaccination rate in boys.

Historically, most oral cancer cases were caused by smoking and heavy drinking and tended to manifest later in life. But even though fewer Americans indulge in these vices today, more of them are engaging in oral sex. Oral cancer rates have risen and begun showing up in younger individuals who, sensibly, seem to prefer oral sex to cigarettes. As the Oral Cancer Foundation notes, HPV strain 16 "is conclusively implicated in the increasing incidence of young non-smoking oral cancer patients." If the disease is detected, the survival rate for HPV-related oral cancer is higher than for the alcohol- and tobacco-correlated versions. But HPV-related cases are often harder to catch because the disease occurs deeper in the mouth (the base of the tongue is a common location), and the warning signs are not as obvious.

There are, of course, HPV vaccines, which the CDC [Centers for Disease Control and Prevention] describes as "very effective" and "very safe." [Pharmaceutical manufacturer] Merck released another study in October [2012] that found that Gardasil, the company's [HPV] vaccine, may cause fainting and brief skin irritation but "no link with more serious health problems was found." The Gardasil vaccine defends against four HPV strains: 6 and 11, which cause 90 percent of genital warts; and 18 and 16, which are linked to cancer. It is FDA [US Food and Drug Administration]-approved and CDC-recommended for males and females. Cervarix defends against the same two cancer-causing strains and a few other lesser culprits. It is not licensed for men. Most insurance companies and public health programs will cover the cost of the HPV shots for those who fall between the FDA-licensed ages of 9 through 26 years old.

But while both vaccines successfully defend against various strains of HPV, only Gardasil has been specifically tested and proven to protect against vulvar, vaginal, and anal cancers as well as cervical cancer. The vaccines' preventive abilities have not been proven for other cancers, which prevents the companies from advertising the vaccines' usefulness against the most prevalent danger: HPV-related oral disease. As the CDC notes: "It is likely that this vaccine also protects men from other HPV-related cancers, like cancers of the penis and oropharynx (back of throat, including base of tongue and tonsils), but there are no vaccine studies that have evaluated these outcomes." Last year the National Cancer Institute [NCI] declined to fund proposed clinical trials on the efficacy of the vaccines for oral cancer, possibly due to budgetary constraints. (NCI officials were not able to respond before publication.)

"The very low rate at which boys are vaccinated is a result of the inability of the manufacturers and doctors to speak openly and with factual evidence about oral cancer in a context that parents will understand," says Brian Hill, president of the Oral Cancer Foundation, who was present at the National Institute of Health meeting where the aid was requested. He says more data and publicity for the vaccines could improve the vaccination rate in boys, which in 2010 was only 1.4 percent. "Vaccination is not just about cervical cancers but cancers their sons will potentially get in the future."

The Dangers of HPV

The dangers of HPV may sound pretty disturbing, particularly for those who might have shrugged off the virus's threat because they believed it wouldn't imperil them or their children. But there are a few important things to understand about HPV. First, we aren't all doomed. A lot of scary statistics get batted around about HPV—6 million new infections a year! Half of sexually active people will get it in their lives!—but most of the 130-plus strains appear to do no damage, and most people's immune systems recognize the handful of dangerous strains as something nasty that should be destroyed.

Vaccinating people after a long sexual history simply isn't worth the cost, from a public health perspective.

But an unlucky 1 percent of the population will not produce the antibodies necessary to defeat the invaders. And it is basically impossible to know whether you or one of your partners is part of that 1 percent. There isn't a reliable blood test to tell whether your body is making antibodies against the virus and is thus protected naturally and you don't need the vaccine.

The vaccines work best in those who have never had sex and therefore have never been exposed to any strain of the virus. That means the safety and efficacy of the vaccines are of limited comfort to those who were sexually active prior to 2006, when the vaccine first became available to females (in 2009 males were officially given the OK).

The Age of Vaccination

After a certain age, 26 in the United States, it is assumed most people have had enough sexual partners that they have been exposed to HPV and their bodies have produced the antibodies necessary to defeat it on their own. In the case of women who have been exposed and developed an infection, it is thought that cervical abnormalities will have been detected and dealt with. Vaccinating people after a long sexual history simply isn't worth the cost, from a public health perspective.

But age isn't always a reliable measure of sexual activity, particularly for those who, say, married young and are getting a divorce and re-entering the dating scene. "If you vaccinate a 45-year-old woman who hasn't had a cervical HPV, the vaccine will work for her as well," says Aimée R. Kreimer of the National Cancer Institute. One study shows the vaccines, which guard against multiple varieties of the virus, can be effective in older women who have not been previously exposed to all of the targeted strains. Another study even suggests that the vaccine prevents further HPV outbreaks among women who have already been treated for cervical infection. "Our findings clearly show that those who have the disease can be protected from new disease and dispels the myth that only young and virgin girls can benefit from the vaccine," says Elmar A. Joura of the Medical University of Vienna and an author of a study published last year in the *British Medical Journal*. "The earlier you vaccinate the better, but the benefit never really stops. It prevents new infections for sure, independent of age."

Unfortunately, the decision about whether to get vaccinated or not isn't a simple one. Gardasil and Cervarix have no therapeutic properties, and once someone has caught one of the strains, the vaccine is no longer protective against that particular infection. There is no reliable blood test to show which HPV strains someone has been exposed to, so it is always possible that the vaccine could be beneficial—or not. But overall, the longer someone has been sexually active, the less likely the vaccine will be of use, which is why public health campaigns focus on the young.

Most nations with universal health care also have rigorous cost-control measures and do not cover the HPV vaccine for people in their 20s. The exact age varies: In the United Kingdom vaccinations are free for those 11 to 17 years old. In Canada, where vaccination programs are run by the provinces, free shots are chiefly available to school-aged women. The same is true in most European nations. Studies like Joura's have inspired many countries to raise their age recommendations beyond America's 9 to 26 years old—Canada suggests the vaccine for women up to the age of 45—but those who aren't covered by the public vaccination programs have to pay for it themselves. "This [hypothetical older] woman is probably not cost-effective in a vaccination program, but when she is looking for the personal benefit she clearly gets it," Joura says.

America's patchwork of private and public providers are often more generous with free vaccinations than are health care systems in other developed nations. Many insurance companies will cover the cost of the shots for those up to the age of 26, as will many publicly funded programs for children, and in some states adults, without private insurance.

Due to our long history of anti-vaccine hysteria, . . . HPV vaccination rates in the United States are terribly low.

The Decision to Get the Vaccine

The FDA's age-licensing limitations or the CDC's age recommendations do not mean that it is a bad idea for those older than 26 to get the HPV vaccine. But the cost of the vaccine in most cases has to be paid out of pocket, to the tune of about $390 to $500. Is it worth it? That's a personal judgment call. The fewer sexual partners you've had, the less likely it is that you've already been exposed to the HPV strains the vaccine defends against. If you anticipate having new partners (potentially with new virus strains you haven't been exposed to before), you may well still benefit from the vaccine.

For people who haven't encountered all of the HPV strains in the vaccine, says Alex Ferenczy of McGill University, "the efficacy of the vaccine is still outstanding for those remaining virus types to which they were not exposed before the vaccination."

One more reason to consider the vaccine is that it is unclear whether antibodies, either induced by an actual HPV infection or the vaccine, have a half-life. That means protection may not last forever. This is true of other antibodies: The immunity conferred by a childhood brush with chickenpox may not last to protect us from shingles, which is caused by the same virus, later in life. It is known that vaccine-induced antibodies or those produced naturally in reaction to an HPV infection last 10 years. But they have not been proven to last a lifetime. If they don't last, this is another possible reason why the vaccine could be effective in women in their 40s, but there is not enough research to prove or disprove this premise.

The vaccine is most useful for young people who are least likely to have been exposed. But by this measure, America is failing. Due to our long history of anti-vaccine hysteria, and sonic conservative politicians' perennial efforts to politicize anything remotely related to sex, HPV vaccination rates in the United States are terribly low. Only 32 percent of girls ages 13 to 17 have received the full three-shot regimen, which is significantly less than in Canada, Great Britain, and some regions of Mexico (although much of the European Union has similarly dismal rates). Like most health issues in the United States, HPV's worst consequences are unequally distributed, with cervical, anal, and penile cancer rates all higher among lower-income populations who tend to be poorly covered by insurance programs and have less access to health care.

For those who are under 26, getting vaccinated will likely be free. Since it is impossible to know how effective the vaccine may be in your case, it's worth getting—it won't hurt you or your wallet. For those over 26, vaccination can be an expensive decision, but it may well be worth it, particularly if you haven't had many sexual partners or are expecting new ones. But to get the most bang for our public health buck, America needs to muster the political will to establish HPV vaccination programs for schoolchildren, both boys and girls. We already require vaccination of children against another sexually transmitted infection before they enter school: hepatitis B. HPV vaccination is an easy and safe way to spare kids a lot of pain and fear later in life.

12

HPV Vaccine Should Require Parental Consent

Wesley J. Smith

Wesley J. Smith authors the blog Human Exceptionalism *at Na-tional Review Online and is a senior fellow at the Discovery Institute's Center on Human Exceptionalism.*

The risk of disease from the sexually transmitted human papillo-mavirus (HPV) does not justify a government mandate that schoolchildren receive the vaccine against it. Although HPV sometimes causes cancer and the vaccine must be given prior to the age of sexual activity to be most effective, it is not in the same category as other vaccines mandated for schoolchildren. Pa-rental rights should be upheld and, although the vaccine should be recommended, it should not be mandated.

Governor Perry's executive order requiring all girls (I think at age 12) to receive the HPV vaccine—with a parental opt out—has become a legitimate political issue in the Repub-lican primary, and I think, nationally. Representative Bach-mann charged Perry with "crony capitalism"—which we need not deal with here—and made the ludicrous and reckless claim that the vaccine can cause retardation. But Megan Mc-Cardle over at *The Atlantic*, breezes past those issues, and in a thoughtful column, gets to the ultimate question: How much power should the state have in a free society to force children to receive the HPV vaccine? First, she points out that thousands of women die each year from cervical cancer, a malady that is often caused by HPV (about 70%). True. She also points out that HPV has caused throat and neck cancers, implying that it can be spread through oral sexual behavior. True again, as I have discussed here at SHS. The primary purpose, she says isn't to protect the vaccinated person but his or her sexual partners. I wouldn't put it that way, but the point she is making is that the vaccine not only protects the person who will not be infected, but also those who might have been infected by that person but for he or she receiving the HPV vaccine. Thus, as in all vaccines, it both keeps people from getting infected by the virus, and if they are not infected, they can't spread it. Allow me to add, the vaccine does not work if a person is already infected, and since the virus is spread sexually, if it is provided before the child becomes sexually active, it is more likely to actually prevent HPV infection. The vaccine is very effective with an extremely low—but importantly for our discussion, not nonexistent—potential for serious side effects. (For example, disability has been reported in connection with the vaccine, as well as Guillain-Barré syndrome, but no causality has yet been demonstrated.) Given these factors, McCardle advocates that the vaccine should be mandatory. From her column:

> Now, maybe you think that this wasn't compelling enough to mandate the vaccine. As it happens I disagree—I think that preventing the transmission of communicable disease is a clear public health issue, and that frankly if this wasn't an STD, no one would even be questioning whether we should vaccinate for a disease that kills at least 3,000 people a year—more than died of measles in the late 1950s, by the way. And of course, thousands more have to go through invasive tests and treatments.

If McCardle is right, all children should receive the vaccine, not just girls. Indeed, I saw a Merck ad the other day urging parents to have their sons inoculated to protect his future sexual partners. But should it be mandatory? We force children to have vaccines against measles, chicken pox, mumps, etc., or not go to school—even though there is a very minor risk of serious side effects—not autism!—precisely because they are readily communicable, in the sense of being spread by air or touch. HPV isn't. That is a crucial distinction, I think. The state interest in preventing a future sexually transmitted disease, which most people will not contract in any event, is therefore less compelling. *Hence, I think the proper approach is to recommend inoculation, but not require it.* I can even get behind an opt-in system in which the vaccine is made available in the nurse's office at school if parents want their kid to have it, but not an opt-out system, in which kids are vaccinated automatically unless the parent says no. But the culture wars are not irrelevant here. I believe there are some advocates who want teenagers to be treated as if they were adults—that is freed from parental oversight—particularly with regard to sexuality. I'll even be more blunt. I think some in society *want* teenagers to have sex: (I mean, other than teenagers). Mandatory HPV inoculation would serve that cultural purpose. Indeed, some even want it provided without parental knowledge along the same line as we've seen with abortion and birth control. No wonder some parents object. That point aside, when it comes to medical issues, parents should be in control of their children's health care absent a compelling state interest. The HPV threat doesn't rise to that level of concern. No forced HPV vaccinations, and no vaccinations without parental knowledge and consent. The cartoons that accompany this post show how the issue paradoxically cuts both ways—enriching a fat cat drug company on one hand, and mocking uptight Christian parents worried about their kids having sex on the other. But for me, it boils down simply to a matter of parental rights.

13

An HIV Vaccine Is Crucial to Attaining an AIDS-Free Generation

Anthony S. Fauci

Anthony S. Fauci is a scientist and director of the National Institute of Allergy and Infectious Diseases at the National Institutes of Health, part of the US Department of Health and Human Services.

The goal of achieving an AIDS-free generation is now within reach, where virtually no one is born with HIV, the risk of being infected with HIV is low, and those with HIV will have treatment to prevent the development of AIDS. Although existing treatment and prevention tools are important in achieving this goal, an HIV vaccine is crucial to realizing it quicker and with more effectiveness.

Because of the extraordinary progress in the fight against HIV/AIDS, we can now consider a question that just a few years ago seemed far-fetched. No longer is it whether we can achieve an AIDS-free generation. Now, the question is: How long will it take and will it be sustained? Vaccines historically have played an important role in the control and even elimination of global health scourges such as smallpox, polio and measles. So two important questions regarding an AIDS-free generation are: Is an HIV vaccine needed to reach this goal, and if so, what role will it play?

An AIDS-Free Generation

An AIDS-free generation would mean that virtually no child is born with HIV; that, as those children grow up, their risk of becoming infected is far lower than it is today; and that those who become infected can access treatment to help prevent them from developing AIDS and from passing the virus on to others.

While the road to an AIDS-free generation will be long and arduous, recent progress in HIV/AIDS prevention and treatment has been encouraging. Initiatives such as the U.S. President's Emergency Plan for AIDS Relief (PEPFAR) and the Global Fund to Fight AIDS, Tuberculosis and Malaria are channeling antiretroviral treatment to millions of people in hard-hit countries. Of the estimated 34 million people worldwide infected with HIV, more than 10 million have access to antiretroviral drugs. Treatment reduces the levels of virus in infected individuals, benefiting their health and lessening the chances that they will transmit the virus to others.

Reaching our goal depends on expanding antiretroviral treatment and proven HIV/AIDS-prevention tools to all people who need them.

Thirteen countries receiving PEPFAR funds have reached a key "tipping point" at which the annual increase in new patients on antiretroviral treatment exceeds the annual number of new HIV infections. The curve of new HIV infections in many countries is trending downward.

The Challenge of Relying on Existing Treatment

Mathematical models suggest that, by implementing existing HIV/AIDS treatment and prevention tools much more broadly worldwide, we can reach an AIDS-free generation. But without an effective HIV vaccine, reaching that goal will take much longer and will be more difficult, and along the way more people will become infected and more lives will be lost.

So while it may be possible, and even likely, to achieve an AIDS-free generation without it, an effective HIV vaccine would get us to an AIDS-free generation faster and, more important, help sustain that accomplishment.

Reaching our goal depends on expanding antiretroviral treatment and proven HIV/AIDS-prevention tools to all people who need them. In this regard, success or failure rests heavily on human behavior. To attain and sustain an AIDS-free generation, those who are already infected or at risk of infection must faithfully practice recommended treatment and/or prevention strategies: taking antiretroviral drugs daily as prescribed; using a condom every time they have sex; and, for those who inject drugs, always using a clean needle and syringe.

The Importance of an AIDS Vaccine

In clinical trials, adherence to an intervention regimen has been shown time and again to be the make-or-break variable in whether that strategy proved effective. Less-than-optimal adherence to a particular regimen reduces the effectiveness of most non-vaccine prevention tools. The chance of acquiring or transmitting HIV increases proportionately the less one sticks to the regimen in question.

Contrast this to an HIV vaccine. For it to be effective, a person probably would need to receive a small number of recommended immunizations, possibly just one. Beyond that, human behavior does not affect the intrinsic effectiveness. Furthermore, unlike with polio, measles or other life-saving vaccines, which are sufficient in themselves to control the spread of the respective disease, an HIV vaccine would stand together with other HIV/AIDS prevention modalities in a new model for infectious diseases. It would be one component, rather than the only component, of a prevention tool kit. We aspire to create a highly effective HIV vaccine. But to be useful, an HIV vaccine need only hit that sweet spot—perhaps 50 percent to 70 percent effective—that, when combined with other prevention tools, provides a highly effective prevention strategy.

Research continues to yield clues to how we might rationally design an effective HIV vaccine, yet many scientific challenges remain. When we do succeed, an HIV vaccine will be the main driver to not only accelerate the decline of new HIV infections—and to do so more efficiently and cost-effectively—but also to maintain an AIDS-free generation once we get there. While an HIV vaccine will be integral to achieving an AIDS-free generation, it also will be essential to realizing our ultimate goal: a world permanently without HIV/AIDS.

14

A New HIV Vaccine Shows Promise—but It Won't Be a Silver Bullet

Mark Joseph Stern

Mark Joseph Stern is a writer for Slate.

Although there is promising research for the development of an HIV vaccine, current research shows limited effectiveness. Instead of relying on an HIV vaccine as a cure-all, there needs to be more reliance on the tools available today. Studies show that circumcision is more effective against HIV than the flu vaccine is against influenza. Sex education, condom use, HIV testing, and medication are all tools that can be implemented now, rather than waiting for a vaccine.

Researchers at Western University in Ontario, Canada, announced today [September 5, 2013] that a newly developed HIV vaccine passed the first phase of clinical trials. That's extremely good news, of course, but it should still be approached with a healthy dose of caution. The announcement doesn't mean that scientists have discovered an effective vaccine against HIV—and even if they had, such a tool would be far from a silver bullet in the fight against AIDS.

The Effectiveness of an HIV Vaccine

If Western University's vaccine actually works, it will, without a doubt, change the face of HIV prevention. A vaccine for the virus has been famously elusive; every trial thus far has failed, some disappointingly, some disastrously. The most effective trial produced a vaccine that's just 31 percent effective, a figure low enough to make further trials impracticable. The worst, without a doubt, ended just last April [2013], when doctors discovered that their vaccine might *increase* patients' risk of contracting the disease.

So a vaccine whose effectiveness matched even, say, that of a flu shot (about 60 percent) would be a big deal. But the effectiveness of Western University's vaccine remains a giant question mark, as researchers took the relatively unorthodox route of testing their shot on already-infected patients. The trial produced encouraging preliminary results: HIV-positive patients began producing exponentially more antibodies to attack HIV-related antigens. In other words, the vaccine kick-started patients' immune systems, provoking them to fight back against a virus they would normally succumb to. And it did so without producing any adverse effects. That's certainly auspicious. But it doesn't necessarily follow that the vaccine will be as effective in preventing HIV-negative people from acquiring the virus. That question will be tested in the trial's next phases.

In the meantime, it's best to remain wary of purported HIV cure-alls. Every few months, doctors and scientists announce a purported cure for HIV: flooding newborns with antiretrovirals, say, or transplanting bone marrow. As a rule, these remedies are limited or one-off—not everyone has the luxury of a bone-marrow transplant, after all—but researchers can't resist extrapolating upon their implications for the broader population. (How often are we told there will be a cure within months?)

The Tools Available Today

That's an understandable impulse, given how discouraging the field of HIV research can otherwise be. But trumpeting such announcements and speculating about their sweeping implications often distracts from more concrete and practical developments in the field. To wit: There is already a vaccine more effective than the flu shot at preventing HIV. It's called circumcision. Research suggests circumcision reduces the risk of HIV acquisition by 60 to 70 percent over the course of one's lifetime (if you're straight, at least)—unlike a condom, which must be used properly during every sexual encounter. And while HIV-prevention circumcision drives are catching on in Africa, the circumcision rate in the United States is dropping dramatically. (This phenomenon is due in part to angry, though discredited, "intactivists.")

Moreover, simple, commonsense measures to prevent HIV transmission like comprehensive sex education remain depressingly controversial in the United States. Americans who have received actual sex ed are significantly more likely to take measures to prevent HIV infection as compared to those who have received abstinence-only education. Yet many public schools are prohibited by conservative legislators from teaching basic HIV-prevention methods like condom use. Similarly controversial is HIV testing, which retains a stigma that dissuades Americans from learning their status. As my colleague Daniel Engber recently argued, we already have therapies that are "good enough to win the war on AIDS" through proper medication. But they rely on everyone learning their HIV status as early as possible—a sadly distant goal for our squeamish populous.

A world equipped with an HIV vaccine would unquestionably be a world with less HIV. But HIV prevention is a complex, multifaceted field, and it's unwise to ignore the real solutions of today in favor of the possible miracles of tomorrow. If Western University's vaccine is truly effective—and we do not yet have proof that it is—millions of people will likely avoid contracting the virus. But millions of people could also avoid it, and treat it properly, by using the tools available at this moment. We shouldn't let the steady stream of purported breakthroughs divert our attention from the work at hand.

Organizations to Contact

The editors have compiled the following list of organizations concerned with the issues debated in this book. The descriptions are derived from materials provided by the organizations. All have publications or information available for interested readers. The list was compiled on the date of publication of the present volume; names, addresses, phone and fax numbers, and e-mail and Internet addresses may change. Be aware that many organizations take several weeks or longer to respond to inquiries, so allow as much time as possible.

Association of American Physicians and Surgeons (AAPS)
1601 N Tucson Blvd., Suite 9, Tucson, AZ   85716-3450
(800) 635-1196 • fax: (520) 325-4230
e-mail: aaps@aapsonline.org
website: www.aapsonline.org

The Association of American Physicians and Surgeons is a national association of physicians dedicated to preserving freedom in the one-on-one patient-physician relationship. AAPS fights in the courts for the rights of patients and physicians, sponsors seminars for physicians, testifies on invitation before committees in Congress, and educates the public. Among the news briefs and publications available at the AAPS website are a fact sheet on mandatory vaccines and the organization's resolution concerning mandatory vaccines.

Centers for Disease Control and Prevention (CDC)
1600 Clifton Rd., Atlanta, GA   30333
(800) 232-4636
e-mail: cdcinfo@cdc.gov
website: www.cdc.gov

The Centers for Disease Control and Prevention, a part of the US Department of Health and Human Services, is the primary federal agency for conducting and supporting public health activities in the United States. Through research and education, the CDC is dedicated to protecting health and promoting quality of life through the prevention and control of disease, injury, and disability. Among the many publications available at the CDC's website regarding vaccines and immunizations are childhood, adolescent, and adult immunization schedules; information about reasons to vaccinate and the importance of vaccinating; and vaccine safety reports, including access to the Vaccine Adverse Event Reporting System (VAERS).

History of Vaccines
19 S 22nd St., Philadelphia, PA   19103-3097
website: www.historyofvaccines.org

History of Vaccines is an educational website created by the College of Physicians of Philadelphia to provide a living chronicle of the history of vaccination. The History of Vaccines site aims to increase public knowledge and understanding of the ways in which vaccines, toxoids, and passive immunization work; how they have been developed; and the role they have played in the improvement of human health. The website includes timelines, articles, and activities on the topic of vaccines.

Immunization Action Coalition (IAC)
1573 Selby Ave., Suite 234, St. Paul, MN   55104
(651) 647-9009 • fax: (651) 647-9131
e-mail: admin@immunize.org
website: www.immunize.org

Immunization Action Coalition works to increase immunization rates and prevent disease. IAC creates and distributes educational materials and facilitates communication about the safety, efficacy, and use of vaccines within the broad immunization community of patients, parents, healthcare organizations, and government health agencies. IAC publishes numerous brochures and vaccination schedules, including the brochure "What If You Don't Immunize Your Child?"

Institute for Vaccine Safety (IVS)

Johns Hopkins Bloomberg School of Public Health
615 N Wolfe St., Room W5041, Baltimore, MD 21205
(410) 955-2955 • fax: (410) 502-6733
e-mail: info@hopkinsvaccine.org
website: www.vaccinesafety.edu

The Institute for Vaccine Safety is an organization within the Johns Hopkins Bloomberg School of Public Health whose goal is to provide an independent assessment of vaccines and vaccine safety. IVS offers a forum for dissemination of data regarding specific issues concerning the safety of immunizations, investigates safety questions, and conducts research. IVS sponsors academic publications, provides information about state school vaccination law exemptions, and provides information on vaccine legislation.

International AIDS Vaccine Initiative (IAVI)

110 William St., Floor 27, New York, NY 10038-3901
(212) 847-1111
website: www.iavi.org

The International AIDS Vaccine Initiative is a global nonprofit organization working to ensure the development of preventive AIDS vaccines. IAVI works with partners in twenty-five countries to research, design, and develop AIDS vaccine candidates. IAVI publishes *VAX* and *IAVI Report*, and several other publications dealing with the AIDS vaccine are available on its website.

National Network for Immunization Information (NNii)

301 University Blvd., Galveston, TX 77555-0350
(702) 200-0201 • fax: (409) 772-5208
e-mail: dipineda@utmb.edu
website: www.immunizationinfo.org

The National Network for Immunization Information is an affiliation of the Infectious Diseases Society of America, the Pediatric Infectious Diseases Society, the American Academy of Pediatrics, the American Nurses Association, the American Academy of Family Physicians, the National Association of Pediatric Nurse Practitioners, the American College of Obstetricians and Gynecologists, the University of Texas Medical Branch, the Society for Adolescent Medicine, and the American Medical Association. NNii provides the public, health professionals, policymakers, and the media with up-to-date information related to immunization to help them understand the issues and make informed decisions. NNii publishes numerous briefs, papers, and pamphlets, including "Exemptions from Immunization Laws," available at its website.

National Vaccine Information Center (NVIC)
21525 Ridgetop Circle, Suite 100, Sterling, VA   20166
(703) 938-0342 • fax: (571) 313-1268
e-mail: contactNVIC@gmail.com
website: www.nvic.org

The National Vaccine Information Center is dedicated to defending the right to informed consent to medical interventions, and to preventing vaccine injuries and deaths through public education. NVIC provides assistance to those who have suffered vaccine reactions; promotes research to evaluate vaccine safety and effectiveness; and monitors vaccine research, development, regulation, policymaking and legislation. Many resources are available at NVIC's website, including position papers and articles, among which is "Vaccinations? Know the Risks and Failures."

Thinktwice Global Vaccine Institute
PO Box 9638, Santa Fe, NM   87504
(505) 983-1856
e-mail: think@thinktwice.com
website: www.thinktwice.com

The Thinktwice Global Vaccine Institute was established in 1996 to provide parents and other concerned people with educational resources enabling them to make more informed vaccine decisions. The institute encourages an uncensored exchange of vaccine information and supports every family's right to accept or reject vaccines. The Thinktwice Global Vaccine Institute has studies, articles, and books available at its website, including the book *Vaccine Safety Manual for Concerned Families and Health Practitioners.*

Vaccination Liberation

PO Box 457, Spirit Lake, ID   83869-0457
(888) 249-1421
e-mail: info@vaccinetruth.com
website: www.vaclib.org

Vaccination Liberation is part of a national grassroots network dedicated to providing information on vaccinations not often made available to the public so that people can avoid and refuse vaccines. Vaccination Liberation works to dispute claims that vaccines are necessary, safe, and effective; expand awareness of alternatives in health care: preserve the right to abstain from vaccination; and repeal all compulsory vaccination laws nationwide. The organization has various information available at its website, including the article "How to Legally Avoid School Immunizations."

Vaccine Education Center

The Children's Hospital of Philadelphia
34th St. and Civic Center Blvd., Philadelphia, PA   19104
(215) 590-1000
website: www.chop.edu

The Vaccine Education Center at the Children's Hospital of Philadelphia educates parents and healthcare providers about vaccines and immunizations. The Vaccine Education Center provides videos, informational tear sheets, and information on every vaccine. Among the numerous publications available for download at the center's website is "Vaccines and the Immune System."

VaccineEthics.org

University of Pennsylvania Center for Bioethics
3401 Market St., Suite 320, Philadelphia, PA   19104

(215) 898-7136
e-mail: feedback@vaccineethics.org
website: www.vaccineethics.org

VaccineEthics.org is a production of the University of Pennsylvania Center for Bioethics that offers information on ethical issues associated with vaccines and vaccination programs. The center has identified and studied ethical challenges present throughout the vaccine life cycle; organized regional, national, and international meetings; and contributed to the scholarly and public dialogues on vaccine ethics and policy. Available at the organization's website are issue briefs such as "Informed Consent in Vaccination."

Bibliography

Books

Omar Bagasra and Donald Gene Pace	*Immunology and the Quest for an HIV Vaccine: A New Perspective.* Bloomington, IN: AuthorHouse, 2012.
Stephanie Cave and Deborah Mitchell	*What Your Doctor May Not Tell You About Children's Vaccinations.* New York: Wellness Central, 2010.
Archana Chatterjee	*Vaccinophobia and Vaccine Controversies of the 21st Century.* New York: Springer, 2013.
Robert Goldberg	*Tabloid Medicine: How the Internet Is Being Used to Hijack Medical Science for Fear and Profit.* New York: Kaplan, 2010.
Louise Kuo Habakus and Mary Holland	*Vaccine Epidemic: How Corporate Greed, Biased Science, and Coercive Government Threaten Our Human Rights, Our Health, and Our Children.* New York: Skyhorse Publishing, 2011.
J.N. Hays	*The Burdens of Disease: Epidemics and Human Response in Western History.* New Brunswick, NJ: Rutgers University Press, 2009.
Kendall Hoyt	*Long Shot: Vaccines for National Defense.* Cambridge, MA: Harvard University Press, 2011.

Walene James   *The Vaccine Religion: Mass Mind &*
the Struggle for Human Freedom.
Mesa, AZ: Dandelion Books, 2011.

Mark A. Largent   *Vaccine: The Debate in Modern*
America. Baltimore, MD: Johns
Hopkins University Press, 2012.

Gary Matsumoto   *Vaccine A: The Covert Government*
Experiment That's Killing Our
Soldiers—and Why GI's Are Only the
First Victims. New York: Basic Books,
2010.

Seth Mnookin   *The Panic Virus: A True Story of*
Medicine, Science, and Fear. New
York: Simon & Schuster, 2011.

Paul A. Offit   *Deadly Choices: How the Anti-Vaccine*
Movement Threatens Us All. New
York: Basic Books, 2011.

Robert W. Sears   *The Vaccine Book: Making the Right*
Decision for Your Child. New York:
Little, Brown, 2011.

Andrew J.   *Callous Disregard: Autism and*
Wakefield   *Vaccine—The Truth Behind a Tragedy.*
New York: Skyhorse Publishing, 2010.

Karie Youngdahl   *The History of Vaccines.* Philadelphia,
et al.   PA: The College of Physicians of
Philadelphia, 2013.

Periodicals and Internet Sources

Peter Bearman   "The Roots of the Vaccine Panic,"
American Prospect, March 5, 2011.
www.prospect.org.

Ari Brown   "Clear Answers & Smart Advice About Your Baby's Shots," Immunization Action Coalition, September 2013. www.immunize.org.

Shannon Brownlee and Jeanne Lenzer   "Does the Vaccine Matter?," *Atlantic*, November 2009.

John E. Calfee   "Junk Science and the Anti-Vaccine Fraud," *American*, January 11, 2011. www.american.com.

Committee on Infectious Diseases   "Policy Statement Recommendation for Mandatory Influenza Immunization of All Healthcare Personnel," *Pediatrics*, October 2010.

Theodore Dalrymple   "The World Before Vaccines Is Too Easy to Forget," *Times*, September 30, 2009.

Leslie Donald   "A Nose Rinse Might Be as Good as a Flu Shot," *Record*, November 13, 2009.

Gary L. Freed et al.   "Parental Vaccine Safety Concerns in 2009," *Pediatrics*, April 2010.

Amanda Gardner   "Fear of Vaccines Has a Long, Persistent History," *HealthDay*, January 26, 2011. www.healthday.com.

Eben Harrell   "Do Flu Vaccines Really Work? A Skeptic's View," *Time*, February 27, 2010.

Jed Lipinski   "Endangering the Herd: The Case for
                        Suing Parents Who Don't Vaccinate
                        Their Kids—or Criminally Charging
                        Them," *Slate*, August 13, 2013. www
                        .slate.com.

Amanda Marcotte   "Government Should Mandate the
                        HPV Vaccine," *Slate*, September 21,
                        2011. www.slate.com.

Megan McArdle   "A Shocking Chart on Vaccination,"
                        Atlantic, October 31, 2011.

Henry I. Miller   "It Takes a Herd," *Hoover Digest*, no.
and Gilbert Ross   4, 2011.

Neil Z. Miller   "Overdosed Babies: Are Multiple
                        Vaccines Safe?," Thinktwice Global
                        Vaccine Institute, 2010. www.think
                        twice.com.

Alex Newman   "Millions of Expired Swine-Flu
                        Vaccines to Be Destroyed as Criticism
                        Mounts," *New American*, July 2, 2010.
                        www.thenewamerican.com.

Alex Seitz-Wald   "What's with Rich People Hating
                        Vaccines?," *Salon*, August 14, 2013.
                        www.salon.com.

Jeffrey A. Singer   "Vaccination and Free Choice,"
                        Reason.com, December 17, 2013.

Michael Wagnitz   "Decision Raises Question: What
                        Exactly Is Thimerosal?," *Capital
                        Times*, April 18, 2010.

Margaret Wente   "Autism, Vaccines, and Fear," *Globe and Mail*, February 4, 2010.

Jay Winsten and "Rolling Back the War on Vaccines,"
Emily Serzin   *Wall Street Journal*, February 6, 2013.

Index